BREAD

BREAD

**THE VERY BEST RECIPES FOR LOAVES, ROLLS, KNOTS
AND TWISTS FROM AROUND THE WORLD**

ANNE SHEASBY

DUNCAN BAIRD PUBLISHERS

LONDON

Bread
Anne Sheasby

First published in the United Kingdom
and Ireland in 2013 by
Duncan Baird Publishers, an imprint of
Watkins Publishing Limited
Sixth Floor
75 Wells Street
London W1T 3QH

A member of Osprey Group

Recipes taken from *The Big Book of Bread*,
published by DBP.

Managing Editor: Sarah Epton
Editor: Rachel Connolly
Managing Designer: Manisha Patel
Design: Gail Jones
Photography: William Lingwood, Toby Scott
Food Stylist: Jayne Cross
Prop Stylists: Helen Trent, Lucy Harvey

A CIP record for this book is available from the
British Library

ISBN: 978-1-84899-189-7

10 9 8 7 6 5 4 3 2 1

Typeset in Myriad Pro
Colour reproduction by PDQ, UK
Printed in China

Publisher's note: While every care has been taken
in compiling the recipes for this book, Watkins
Publishing Limited, or any other persons who
have been involved in working on this publication,
cannot accept responsibility for any errors or
omissions, inadvertent or not, that may be found
in the recipes or text, nor for any problems that
may arise as a result of preparing one of these
recipes. If you are pregnant or breastfeeding or
have any special dietary requirements or medical
conditions, it is advisable to consult a medical
professional before following any of the recipes
contained in this book.

UNLESS OTHERWISE STATED:
• Use large eggs
• Do not mix metric and imperial measurements
• 1 tsp = 5ml • 1 tbsp = 15ml • 1 cup = 250ml
• All recipes serve 4

Contents

Bread basics

Types of bread

Bread comes in all shapes, sizes, colours, textures and flavours and few things beat the aroma of freshly baked bread filling your home. Baking does not have to be time consuming or complicated; by mastering the basic technique of breadmaking, there are endless ways to experiment with recipes and to create delicious home-made breads, from everyday loaves and quick breads to enriched speciality breads, flat breads and gluten-free breads. Plus, the increasing popularity of breadmachines provides the home baker with many additional recipes and ideas.

Basic ingredients for breadmaking

Bread has four essential ingredients: flour, yeast, liquid and salt. Other ingredients such as sugar, fat and eggs may be added to produce different types of bread.

Flour

Types of flour

For traditional yeasted breads, choose strong wheat flour, also known as breadmaking flour or bread flour. It is available in several varieties, the most common being white, brown, wholemeal, granary and soft grain white. Strong or bread flour has a high gluten content, which stretches the dough and traps in air as it cooks, to give a well-shaped loaf with a good rise and a light, open texture.

Strong flour is recommended for use when making bread by hand and also when making bread in a breadmachine. Flours vary between brands but choose organic, unbleached strong flour, if possible. Plain or self-raising flours should only be used in yeast-free breads (although some yeasted doughs use a mixture of flours, such as French Baguettes), and all of the quick bread recipes in this book are made using these types of flour. Quick breads tend to have a closer, more crumbly texture.

Breads made with strong wholemeal flour may take a little longer to rise than those made with white flour, as the bran in wholemeal flour inhibits the gluten. They also tend to be slightly denser and coarser in texture than white breads, though they are very flavourful and nutritious. An alternative idea is to use half strong white and half strong wholemeal flour for a lighter-textured loaf.

Strong brown flour will produce a lighter brown loaf, whereas strong granary or malthouse flour, which is a mixture of strong brown flour and malted wheat flakes or grains, produces loaves with a nutty, malted flavour. Strong granary flour may also be made from a combination of strong wholemeal and white flours, sometimes with rye flour added, and malted wheat grains. Stoneground flour (available in wholemeal and brown varieties) is ground between stones, hence the name, and this gives the flour a slightly roasted, nutty flavour. Strong soft grain flour is strong white flour with kibbled grains of wheat and rye added, and this also produces a tasty loaf.

Other flours such as barley, millet and spelt flours have a low gluten content, but can be combined with strong bread flours to make delicious loaves. Rye flour is also used in breadmaking and although it has a good gluten content, rye doughs are often sticky and difficult to handle, so for this reason it is frequently mixed with other flours to create a more manageable dough.

Gluten-free flours

If you have an intolerance or sensitivity to gluten, then you will need to avoid flours which contain gluten. Because gluten is the protein that strengthens and binds dough in baking, you may need to find alternative binding agents when using gluten-free flours. A combination of starches often works better than a single type, and adding ingredients such as egg, grated apple or mashed banana may also help. It should be noted that gluten-free flours tend to make denser loaves with a closer texture.

A range of gluten-free flours including gluten-free white and bread flours (as well as gluten-free plain flour) are available from many supermarkets or health food stores. Alternatively, you can combine a selection of gluten-free flours yourself. Other naturally gluten-free flours include rice flour, gram (chickpea) flour, buckwheat flour, cornmeal or maize meal flour, tapioca flour and potato flour.

When using gluten-free flours in recipes, it is important to remember that they tend to absorb more liquid than ordinary flours, so you may need to add a little more liquid to all your recipes (we have accounted for this in the recipes in this book), if you are adapting/changing standard recipes into gluten-free recipes.

It is important to remember when making bread by hand or using a breadmachine, that all utensils should be washed thoroughly before and after use, as even the slightest trace of wheat may cause an allergic reaction in someone who suffers with coeliac disease or who has an intolerance to wheat. If you are baking a batch of breads, be careful to keep ingredients separate so that there is no risk of wheat flour contaminating the gluten-free foods. If you do a lot of gluten-free baking, it may be sensible to always use separate baking tins and cooking utensils.

Gluten-free bread mixes are also available from health food shops, and these are suitable for making bread by hand or in the breadmachine. We used Orgran's Easy-Bake Gluten-Free Bread Mix (available in health food shops) for a couple of the recipes in the Gluten-Free Breads chapter.

For all the gluten-free recipes in this book (where applicable), we used Doves Farm range of gluten-free flours (readily available in supermarkets and health food shops), which includes gluten-free plain white flour, gluten-free white bread flour and gluten-free brown bread flour. These all gave excellent results. Some recipes also contain gluten-free self-raising white flour – if this is not available, simply use gluten-free plain white flour and add 1 teaspoon gluten-free baking powder to each 225g (8oz) of plain flour used. Other brands of gluten-free flours are also available.

Yeast

Yeast is an essential ingredient in breadmaking as it causes the bread to rise. It is a living organism, which requires food and moisture to grow and survive. Fresh yeast is alive but inactive when you buy it, and it will only become active once it is mixed with a warm liquid such as milk or water. Dried yeast is also inactive and it will remain so until it becomes activated during the process of fermentation.

Yeast feeds on the sugar and later the starches in the flour and it then releases a gas (carbon dioxide) that makes dough rise. Warmth encourages the yeast to grow more quickly, but it is not essential. Bread dough will rise in a refrigerator overnight and this slow, cool rise produces a good, well-shaped loaf.

Types of yeast

Yeast is available in several different forms including fresh yeast, traditional or ordinary dried active yeast, and easy-blend, easy-bake, quick or fast-action dried yeast. All forms of yeast can be used and interchanged in the recipes, so long as the general guidelines are followed. It is important to treat yeast with care. As soon as it comes into contact with moisture of any kind it will activate and start to feed on the starch and sugars in the dough.

Easy-Blend (Easy-Bake) or Fast-Action (Quick) Dried Yeast Easy-blend (easy-bake) or fast-action (quick) dried yeast is a combination of dried yeast and the bread improver ascorbic acid (vitamin C), which accelerates the action of the yeast during the fermentation process, allowing a quick rise and eliminating the need to 'knock back' the dough and rise it for a second time. This type of yeast is available in handy 6g or 7g (¼oz) sachets, or it can be bought in resealable foil packets of 125g (4½oz), which need to be kept in the refrigerator once opened and used within 10–12 weeks. Easy-blend (easy-bake) or fast-action (quick) dried yeast is sprinkled and mixed directly into the flour or dry ingredients, before adding the warm liquid to make the dough. It is a fast-action yeast, so that often only one kneading and proving (rising) is required, making yeast cookery quicker and easier. It is important to remember that yeast won't work if it is stale, so always follow instructions for storage and adhere to the use-by date on the packet. This type of yeast is recommended for use in a breadmachine.

Traditional or Ordinary Dried Active Yeast Traditional or ordinary dried active yeast is compressed yeast from which the moisture has been removed. It is available in granules. This type of yeast will need to be reactivated with water prior to use. It is usually available in 125g (4½oz) tins and will keep for up to 2 months once opened. Traditional or ordinary dried active yeast is simply blended with warm liquid (with a pinch or so of sugar to help activate it), covered and left in a warm place for about 15 minutes or until a frothy head develops. Once reactivated, it is then used like fresh yeast, to make hand-made breads and doughs which require two rising/proving periods. It is not recommended for use in a breadmachine.

Fresh Yeast Fresh yeast is available to buy in some baker's, health food shops or delicatessens. It should look firm, moist and creamy-coloured and should have a good 'yeasty' smell when you buy it. Fresh yeast is simply blended with the warm water or liquid specified in the recipe and then mixed with the flour to make a dough. It can be kept, wrapped, for up to 3 days in the refrigerator or in the freezer for up to 3 months. Fresh yeast is not suitable for use in a breadmachine.

Sourdough Starter A sourdough starter is another traditional method of leavening, which produces a close-textured loaf with a distinctive flavour. To make a sourdough starter, a mixture of yeast, flour and water is left to ferment for several days before it is added to the dough.

A NOTE ABOUT THE YEAST USED IN THE RECIPES IN THIS BOOK

For this cookbook, in the majority of recipes that contain yeast, we have used easy-blend dried yeast, for convenience and ease of use. This type of dried yeast is simply added straight to the flour, with no need to reconstitute or activate it in water first.

With many of the plainer, more basic bread doughs (which specify using easy-blend dried yeast) we also include two rises. Although this is not necessary when using this type of yeast, it tends to give a better overall result (i.e. the doughs have one rise after the initial kneading and one rise after the dough has been knocked back and shaped, before baking).

There is also a selection of yeasted doughs included in this book that only require one rising, and for these recipes we have specified using fast-action dried yeast (although in fact, easy-blend, easy-bake, quick and fast-action dried yeasts are similar products with different names). This is so that, at a glance, you are able to see if a recipe requires one or two rises.

For many of the enriched or speciality doughs, we have also specified using easy-blend dried yeast and these doughs have two rises. Enriched doughs such as Brioche, Chelsea Buns and Stollen, which contain ingredients such as fat, sugar and/or eggs, take more time to rise than plainer doughs, so this type of dough must be allowed to rise before and after shaping to achieve the best results. However, there is also a small selection of enriched doughs where we have specified using fast-action dried yeast, as these are slightly lighter doughs which require only one rising.

Doughs made using fresh yeast or ordinary dried yeast granules always require two rises to produce bread with a light, even texture. There are some breads, such as Ciabatta, where fresh yeast really gives the best results, but for most of the recipes in this book, you can use easy-blend or fast-action dried yeasts.

As a rough guide, one sachet (6g or 7g/¼oz) of easy-blend or fast-action dried yeast (1 sachet = about 2 teaspoons) is equivalent to 15g (½oz) fresh yeast or 1 tablespoon ordinary dried yeast. This quantity of yeast is enough to rise up to 750g (1lb 10oz) flour.

For doughs enriched with butter, sugar, eggs, fruit, etc, you will usually need to add a little more yeast to ensure a good rise – please refer to the recipes in this book for guidance.

Other leavening agents

While yeast is the most popular and most common leavening ingredient used in breadmaking, other raising agents such as baking powder and bicarbonate of soda are also used for making some breads, including quick breads such as Tomato and Olive Soda Bread and Wheaten Bread.

Sugar and other sweeteners

Sugar helps to feed the yeast and make it more active, hence encouraging fermentation to take place more quickly. Modern types of yeast (such as easy-blend or fast-action dried yeast) no longer need sugar as the flour provides them with enough food, but for good measure it is usual to add a little sugar in breadmaking.

White, light soft brown or dark soft brown sugars can all be used in breadmaking and 1 teaspoon sugar is enough to activate the yeast in a 500g (1lb 2oz) loaf, although more sugar will be added to sweet and some enriched doughs.

In some bread recipes, honey, golden syrup, maple syrup, malt extract, black treacle or molasses are used to add flavour and colour. Sugar also helps delay the staling process in baked bread because it attracts moisture. However, too much sugar can cause the dough to rise too much and collapse, so follow the recipes carefully. Artificial sweeteners are not suitable for breadmaking.

Salt

Salt improves the flavour of bread. However, salt also slows down the action of yeast, so be careful not to add too much, and do not add salt directly to the yeast. Salt helps the dough to rise in a controlled and even way, resulting in a well-risen, even loaf. Too little salt means the loaf will stale more quickly; too much and the crust will harden.

Liquids

The liquid used in breadmaking is usually water, although milk or a mixture of milk and water is used in some recipes. Milk tends to give the bread a softer, lighter texture and a soft crust. The temperature of the liquid used is important. It should be warm (tepid) or hand-hot (about 38°C/100°F); if it is too hot it may destroy the yeast, and if it is too cold it will slow down the action of the yeast.

When adding liquid in a yeasted bread recipe, in many recipes the quantities of liquid given should be used as a guide, because the absorbency of flour varies according to type and brand, and also depends on the surrounding conditions such as heat and humidity. For example, doughs made with wholemeal flours tend to need more liquid than those made with white flour. Always add the liquid gradually, rather than all at once, so that you only add as much as is needed. However, with some yeasted bread recipes, all the liquid needs to be added to the dough to achieve the correct consistency, so always read through the recipe carefully before you begin, as this will be indicated in the text. Other liquids including buttermilk, natural yogurt, coconut milk, beer, cold tea or fruit juices such as orange juice, may also be used to make some bread doughs.

Fats

Some recipes include a little fat, such as butter or lard, to be rubbed into the flour before or after the yeast is added. Other recipes may include the addition of oil or melted butter. We have specified using butter in most of the recipes (where applicable), but in many of these recipes, vegetable margarine or a similar alternative fat may be used instead of butter, if preferred. Fats add flavour to breads as well as improving their keeping qualities, but too much fat will slow down the action of the yeast. Some enriched doughs such as Danish Pastries contain a large amount of fat, which helps to produce these delicious breads and pastries. The rising times on recipes such as these may be a little longer than with basic bread doughs.

Bread mixes

There is a good range of bread mixes available that are ideal for making bread by hand or in a breadmachine, enabling you to make and bake flavourful breads with very little effort. They include white, wholemeal or granary bread mixes as well as a range of flavoured mixes, and speciality bread mixes such as ciabatta or focaccia.

We have used a basic white bread mix for a selection of recipes in this book, to create some tempting, flavourful breads. Once bread mixes have been mixed, kneaded and shaped, they only require one rising, so are ideal if you would like to create a tasty loaf but are a little short of time.

Essential breadmaking techniques for yeasted doughs

Mixing and kneading the dough

Once the yeast and liquid (and sometimes other ingredients, depending on the recipe) have been added to the dry ingredients, they are mixed together to form a soft, pliable dough. The dough then needs to be kneaded vigorously to strengthen and work the gluten in the flour and to create a smooth, stretchy, elastic dough to achieve a good rise. Kneading is vital for good, even-textured, well-shaped bread and it ensures that the yeast is distributed throughout the dough so that the loaf rises evenly. Remember, if yeasted dough has not been kneaded it will not rise.

If you are kneading the dough by hand this will usually take about 10 minutes. Turn the dough onto a lightly floured surface and pull and stretch it firmly away from you using the heel of your hand, then fold it towards you, press it down again and away from you using the heel of your hand, giving it a small turn as you do so. Continue pulling, stretching, folding, pressing and turning the dough like this until it becomes smooth and elastic.

Alternatively, you can use a large mixer with a dough hook attachment, or a food processor, to mix and knead the dough for you. Kneading in a mixer (on a low speed) usually only takes about 5 minutes. Many domestic food processors will only allow you to knead moderate amounts of dough at a time. However, be careful not to over-knead the dough if using an electric mixer or food processor, and remember that not all doughs are suitable for kneading in a mixer, e.g. doughs containing dried fruit, where the fruit is added with the flour, may result in the fruit becoming too broken down by the kneading action of the machine.

Rising the dough

Once the dough has been kneaded, place it in a large, lightly oiled bowl (leaving plenty of room for expansion) and cover with a clean tea towel or oiled cling film. This will help the dough to rise and will prevent a skin from forming on the top. Leave in a warm place until the dough has risen and doubled in size and springs back slowly when you press it with your fingertips.

The time dough takes to rise will depend on several factors including the temperature of the room, the temperature of the ingredients, type of recipe, etc. The first rising of bread doughs usually takes the longest, on average between 1–2 hours. Enriched doughs tend to take longer to rise, e.g. the Chocolate Bread recipe takes between 2–3 hours to rise sufficiently. The ideal temperature for rising dough is about 24–27°C/75–80°F – this is a similar temperature to an airing cupboard or near a warm oven. However, don't be tempted to speed up the rising process by putting the dough somewhere hot, as this may kill the yeast and will result in misshapen bread with a poor texture.

Some people prefer to rise their dough more slowly (for example in a cool, unheated room) as they feel cool rising produces a better tasting loaf. Avoid rising dough in a draughty room, though, as this may cause the bread to bake unevenly.

Knocking back and second-rising or proving the dough

Once the dough has risen, it is then 'knocked back'. This process will smooth out any large air pockets and ensure an even texture in the bread. To 'knock back' the dough, remove the cover and punch the risen dough in the bowl with your fist to deflate it and knock out the air. Turn the collapsed dough onto a lightly floured surface and knead it briefly – for about 2–3 minutes – to redistribute the yeast and the gases formed by fermentation. Sometimes, at this stage, other ingredients such as olives, chopped herbs, chopped sun-dried tomatoes, chopped nuts, seeds or dried fruit may be kneaded into the dough.

The dough is then shaped or moulded as required, and then covered once again and left in

a warm place until it has doubled in size. This is known as the second-rising or proving stage; it is quicker than the first rising and usually takes about 30–60 minutes, depending on the recipe.

It is important not to over-prove the dough at this stage, otherwise the bread may collapse during baking – make sure the dough only rises until it is doubled in size. However, if it does not rise enough at this stage the loaf will be dense and flat. To test if the dough has risen enough, simply press it lightly with your fingertip. It should feel springy and the indentation made by your finger should slowly spring back and fill.

For professional-looking bread, proving baskets (often used by professional bakers) may be used for proving the dough. Proving baskets are wicker baskets lined with linen or canvas, which are lightly floured, and they provide extra support to the bread during its final rising. They are available in round or long (baguette) shapes from good kitchenware shops. Once the dough has been proved in a basket, simply turn it out onto a baking sheet and bake as normal.

Shaping bread
Once the bread dough has been knocked back, it may be shaped in various ways. Common bread shapes include traditional tin loaf, cottage loaf, large round or oval, plait or baton, while bread rolls can be shaped into rounds, knots, long rolls and rings etc. Dough can also be slashed with a sharp knife in various ways before or after proving: slash the top of the loaf along its length (this is the traditional finish for a tin loaf); make criss-cross lines over the top of the loaf; cut a deep cross over the centre of the loaf or cut several diagonal slashes across the top of the loaf.

Slashing the tops of loaves is not only done for visual effect but can also be done for practical reasons, to provide escape routes for the air and to control the direction and extent of the rise during baking. The earlier you slash the dough the wider the splits in the baked loaf, and the deeper the slashes the more the bread will open during baking.

Glazing bread

Brushing a loaf with a glaze before baking will enhance the colour of the bread, as well as adding flavour to the crust. Glazes not only help to give the baked bread an attractive finish, they also add moisture to the loaf (by producing steam which helps to expand the loaf and ensure even cooking). Additionally, glazes help toppings, decorations or garnishes to stick to the surface of the dough.

Breads may be glazed before, during or just after baking. The most common ingredients used to glaze loaves are water, milk or beaten egg, but you can also try melted butter, olive oil, single cream, warmed clear honey, sugar syrup or a thin glacé icing for a variety of different finishes.

Finishing touches for bread

Various ingredients can be used for topping or finishing bread before it is baked, and each ingredient will create a different effect. Try sprinkling with seeds, cracked or kibbled wheat, rolled oats, salt flakes, grated cheese or fresh herbs before baking, or dust with a little flour. For sweet breads, try dusting with icing sugar or sprinkling bread with crushed sugar cubes, chopped nuts, flaked almonds, dried fruits or grated or chopped chocolate, usually after baking.

A NOTE ABOUT ENRICHED DOUGHS

During baking, some of the enriched doughs (or doughs containing chocolate, more sugar, etc) in this book may need covering to prevent them browning too much. If the bread shows signs of browning too quickly, simply cover it loosely with foil towards the end of the cooking time.

Storing bread

Most home-made bread is at its best when served freshly baked and on the day it is made, and it should be eaten within 1–2 days as it stales quite quickly. Bread with a high fat or sugar content, such as enriched doughs, are also best eaten when freshly baked, but will keep longer, for up to 2–3 days.

Bread is best stored in a cool, dry, well-ventilated bread bin or an earthenware bread crock, and not in the refrigerator (the cold draws moisture out of the loaf, making it dry and stale). Wrap bread in foil or a plastic bag if it has a soft crust, and in a paper or fabric bag if it is crusty.

Bread also freezes well for a short time – up to about 1 month. Simply seal the bread in a polythene freezer bag, or alternatively, cut the loaf in half or into slices and freeze in convenient portions, ideal for defrosting when required. Defrost frozen breads at room temperature.

Quick (yeast-less) breads tend to stale quickly and these are often best eaten freshly baked and warm from the oven.

Many shop-bought breads contain preservatives or flour improvers, hence they have a longer storage life than home-made breads.

Breadmaking utensils

The various utensils useful for breadmaking are too numerous to mention here, but most modern kitchens will have sufficient equipment to make bread.

A NOTE ABOUT BREAD TINS AND MOULDS

If using a loaf tin or other shaped tin to bake your bread, it is important to choose one that is the right size for the amount of dough you have made. As a general guide, the tin should be about twice the size of the dough.

Traditionally, loaf tins came in two sizes – 450g (1lb) and 900g (2lb). However, nowadays there is a wider choice of loaf tin sizes to choose from. For this book, when we refer to 450g (1lb) and 900g (2lb) loaf tins we have used tins with the following approximate dimensions (the measurements are the *internal* measurements of each tin):

450g (1lb) loaf tin = 18½cm (7¼in) = length; 9cm (3½in) = width; 5.5cm (2¼in) = depth
900g (2lb) loaf tin = 22cm (8½in) = length; 11cm (4¼in) = width; 7cm (2¾in) = depth

We also occasionally use a slightly larger (Continental) 1.1kg (2½lb) loaf tin in some recipes, with the following approximate *internal* measurements:

1.1kg (2½lb) loaf tin = 25cm (10in) = length; 11cm (4¼in) = width; 7.5cm (3in) = depth

We have used several other tins for some of the recipes in this book, such as springform tins, deep, round cake tins, square cake tins and muffin tins, some with loose bases, others not, as well as more specialist shaped tins or moulds such as brioche and kugelhopf tins. We have included the appropriate tin size or capacity in the relevant recipes.

Tins, such as those mentioned above, should be greased before use – simply wiping vegetable oil over the surface with absorbent kitchen paper should suffice. For breads baked on a baking sheet, either grease or flour the baking sheet before use, whichever you prefer. Some high fat recipes such as Danish Pastries are better baked on a greased rather than a floured baking sheet, to avoid sticking. With each recipe, we include instructions on preparing the tins or baking sheets.

Breadmachines

There is a wide range of breadmachines to choose from and selecting a model to suit you will depend on several factors, including size or capacity required and budget. Do some research before buying a breadmachine to ensure it is the right model to suit you.

We have included a whole chapter on breadmachine recipes in this book, but throughout the book we also include a selection of other recipes that are suitable for making both by hand and in the breadmachine.

We have given ingredient quantities and cooking instructions for each breadmachine recipe, but it is very important that you thoroughly read the manufacturer's instruction book for your particular breadmachine before embarking on any of the recipes. Bread machines vary, so, for example, you may find that you have to add the ingredients to the bread pan in a slightly different order to that given in these recipes. You should always add the ingredients to the bread pan in the order specified in your instruction book.

Breadmachines will save time and effort and they are relatively simple to use. Before you begin, it is well worth familiarising yourself with your machine and experimenting with the different settings and options. Practice makes perfect and you will soon master how to use and programme your machine. The names of the settings used, such as Rapid Bake or Basic White, may also differ slightly from one model to another. The delay timer facility is useful for when you are not at home or are asleep – it's hard to beat the aroma of freshly baked bread as you walk through the door at the end of a hard day or when you wake up in the morning!

When making bread in a breadmachine it is vital that the salt, sugar and yeast are kept apart from each other. This is less important if you are making some breads using the Rapid Bake or Fast Bake programme, as the ingredients are mixed as soon as the programme begins.

Bread machine pans vary in size between models and on large models you may have the option of making up to three different sizes of loaf. We have selected a medium-sized loaf for these recipes, which should suit most breadmachines.

Programmes vary between models, but many include a Basic White or Normal, Wholewheat or Wholemeal, Multigrain, Rapid Bake or Fast Bake, Sweet, Raisin Bake or Raisin Beep, Dough Only, Raisin Dough and Bake Only programmes. Some models may also include more specialised programmes such as French, Cake, Sandwich, Pizza and Jam. Again, please refer to your manufacturer's instruction book for more details of the programmes included with your machine

Some machines also offer a choice of three crust colours: light, medium or dark. However, if your machine does not have this option or you would prefer a darker crust once the loaf has been baked, simply brush the top of the baked loaf with a little melted butter or egg yolk mixed with water and brown under a hot grill or in a preheated oven at 200°C/400°F/gas mark 6 for 5–10 minutes.

Adapting recipes for use in a breadmachine

Having mastered your breadmachine, you may decide that you would like to try and adapt some of your own recipes to make in it. There is no easy formula for adapting conventional recipes for the breadmachine, but the best advice is to look through the recipes in this book and find one that is similar and use it as a rough guide. It is also worth checking your manufacturer's instruction book as this may give advice for adapting your own recipes to suit that particular model. Once you have tried a few recipes in your breadmachine, you will soon get the feel for how to adapt your own.

Quick tips for adapting your own recipes

- First, make sure you use the correct quantities for the breadmachine, ensuring that the total quantity of ingredients will fit into your bread pan. Do not exceed the recommended maximum. If necessary, reduce the flour and liquid quantities to match those in a similar recipe.

- Use the flour and water quantities given in the recipes in this book as a guide and always refer to your manufacturer's instruction book. Keep the flour and liquid in the correct proportions. You may find that you need to add a little more water than the amount given in hand-made recipes, but this will vary depending on several factors, such as the type of recipe itself, other ingredients used, etc. With a bit of practice, you will soon get the feel for approximately how much liquid to add to different basic quantities of flour.

- Keep the yeast dry and separate from any liquids added to the pan, until mixing commences. Separate the yeast from the liquid by adding the yeast before or after the flour (or according to your instruction book).

- Always keep salt, sugar, butter and yeast separate from each other until mixing commences.

- Always replace fresh yeast with an appropriate amount of easy-blend (easy-bake) or fast-action (quick) dried yeast (for more details refer to your manufacturer's guidelines). As a rough guide for wholemeal bread, try using 1 teaspoon easy-blend or fast-action dried yeast for up to 375g (13oz) flour or 1½ teaspoons yeast for up to 675g (1½lb) flour.

- If you are using the timer delay setting, use skimmed milk powder and water instead of fresh milk.

- If your conventional recipe uses egg, add the egg as part of the total liquid measurement.

- Check the consistency of the dough during the first few minutes of mixing. Remember that bread machines require a slightly softer dough than with hand-made doughs, so you may need to add a little extra liquid. The dough should be wet enough to gradually relax back. If it is crumbly or the machine seems to be labouring, add a little extra water. If it is sticking to the sides of the pan and doesn't form a ball, add a little extra flour.

Gluten-free breads
When making gluten-free breads in the breadmachine, the Rapid Bake or Fast Bake programme will usually produce the best results. Refer to your manufacturer's guidelines for details of the specific setting(s) recommended for gluten-free breads made in your particular breadmachine.

A NOTE ABOUT THE RECIPES
- Please note that both metric and imperial measurements are given for the recipes. Follow either set of measures, not a mixture of both, as they are not interchangeable.

- All spoon measures are level unless otherwise stated. Sets of measuring spoons are available in metric and imperial for accurate measurements.

- Medium eggs should be used in the recipes, except where otherwise specified.

- We have included cooking temperatures for electric and gas ovens. Remember if you have a fan-assisted oven that you need to reduce the oven temperature slightly (usually by around 20 degrees) and/or adjust the cooking times. Please refer to manufacturer's guidelines for more specific information on adjusting the temperature and time for your cooker, if applicable.

- Some of the recipes in this book may contain raw or lightly cooked eggs – these recipes are not recommended for babies and young children, pregnant mums, the elderly and those convalescing.

Everyday breads

In this chapter you will
find a selection of delicious breads
and rolls that are ideal for regular baking. We
include rustic, homely basics such as Cheddar Twists,
Malted Wholegrain Cobb and Breakfast Rolls, as well
as a collection of slightly more unusual breads – from
Cheese and Poppyseed Plait and Greek Olive Bread
to Spiced Walnut Bread and Bagels – that are
enjoyed all over the world, many
on a daily basis.

Basic white bread

PREPARATION TIME *20 minutes, plus rising* **COOKING TIME** *30–35 minutes*
MAKES *2 loaves (each loaf serves 12–14)*

700g (1lb 9oz) strong plain
white flour

2 teaspoons salt

1 teaspoon caster sugar

1½ teaspoons easy-blend
dried yeast

25g (1oz) butter, diced

about 450ml (16fl oz)
warm water

1 Grease two 900g (2lb) loaf tins and set aside. Sift the flour and salt into a large bowl, stir in the sugar and yeast, then rub in the butter. Make a well in the centre, then add enough warm water, mixing to form a soft dough.

2 Turn the dough onto a lightly floured surface and knead until smooth and elastic. Shape the dough into a round, then place it in a lightly oiled bowl, cover and leave to rise in a warm place until doubled in size.

3 Knock back the dough on a lightly floured surface, then divide it in half and shape each portion into an oblong. Press into the loaf tins, cover and leave to rise again for about 30 minutes, or until doubled in size.

4 Meanwhile, preheat the oven to 230°C/450°F/gas mark 8. Bake the loaves for 15 minutes, then reduce the oven temperature to 200°C/400°F/gas mark 6 and bake for a further 15–20 minutes, or until the bread is risen, golden brown and sounds hollow when tapped underneath. Turn out and cool on a wire rack. Serve in slices.

Variation *If you do not have any suitable loaf tins, simply shape the knocked-back dough into a large round or oval (or divide the dough in half and shape each portion into a round or oval), place on a greased baking sheet, leave to rise, then bake as above.*

Basic wholemeal bread

PREPARATION TIME *20 minutes, plus rising*   COOKING TIME *30–35 minute*
MAKES *2 loaves (each loaf serves 12–14)*

225g (8oz) strong plain white flour

450g (1lb) strong plain wholemeal flour

2 teaspoons salt

1 teaspoon caster sugar

2 teaspoons easy-blend dried yeast

25g (1oz) butter, diced

about 450ml (16fl oz) warm water

1 Grease two 900g (2lb) loaf tins and set aside. Sift the white flour into a large bowl, then stir in the wholemeal flour, salt, sugar and yeast. Rub the butter into the flour mixture. Make a well in the centre, then add enough warm water, mixing to form a soft dough.

2 Turn the dough onto a lightly floured surface and knead until smooth and elastic. Shape the dough into a round, then place it in a lightly oiled bowl, cover and leave to rise in a warm place until doubled in size.

3 Knock back the dough on a lightly floured surface, then divide it in half and shape each portion into an oblong. Press into the loaf tins, cover and leave to rise again for about 30 minutes, or until doubled in size.

4 Meanwhile, preheat the oven to 230°C/450°F/gas mark 8. Bake the loaves for 15 minutes, then reduce the oven temperature to 200°C/400°F/gas mark 6 and bake for a further 15–20 minutes, or until the bread is risen, lightly browned and sounds hollow when tapped underneath. Turn out and cool on a wire rack. Serve in slices.

Malted wholegrain cobb

PREPARATION TIME *20 minutes, plus rising*   **COOKING TIME** *30–35 minutes*
MAKES *1 large loaf (serves 14–16)*

450g (1lb) strong granary flour

225g (8oz) strong plain wholemeal flour

2 teaspoons salt

25g (1oz) butter, diced

2 teaspoons easy-blend dried yeast

150ml (¼ pint) warm milk, plus extra for glazing

2 tablespoons malt extract

about 300ml (½ pint) warm water

kibbled or cracked wheat, for sprinkling

1 Grease or flour a baking sheet and set aside. Mix the flours and salt in a large bowl, then rub in the butter. Stir in the yeast. Make a well in the centre, then add the milk, malt extract and enough warm water, mixing to form a soft dough.

2 Turn the dough onto a lightly floured surface and knead until smooth and elastic. Shape the dough into a round, then place it in a lightly oiled bowl, cover and leave to rise in a warm place until doubled in size.

3 Knock back the dough on a floured surface and shape into a large round. Place on the baking sheet, cover and leave to rise again for about 30 minutes, or until doubled in size.

4 Meanwhile, preheat the oven to 230°C/450°F/gas mark 8. Using a sharp knife, slash the top of the loaf into a cross shape, brush with a little milk and sprinkle with kibbled wheat.

5 Bake for 10 minutes, then reduce the oven temperature to 200°C/400°F/gas mark 6 and bake for a further 20–25 minutes, or until the bread is risen, lightly browned and sounds hollow when tapped underneath. Transfer to a wire rack to cool. Serve in slices.

Cottage loaf

PREPARATION TIME *20 minutes, plus rising* COOKING TIME *30–35 minutes*
MAKES *1 large loaf (serves 14–16)*

700g (1lb 9oz) strong plain white flour, plus extra for dusting

2 teaspoons salt

25g (1oz) butter, diced

1 sachet (7g/¼oz) easy-blend dried yeast

1 teaspoon caster sugar

about 400ml (14fl oz) warm water

beaten egg, to glaze

1 Grease or flour 2 baking sheets and set aside. Sift the flour and salt into a large bowl, then rub in the butter. Stir in the yeast and sugar. Make a well in the centre, then add enough water, mixing to form a fairly firm dough. To ensure a good-shaped cottage loaf, the bread dough for this recipe needs to be firm enough so that the bottom round of dough can support the weight of the top piece of dough without sagging. However, if you do end up with a misshapen loaf, don't worry, it will still taste delicious!

2 Turn the dough onto a lightly floured surface and knead until smooth and elastic. Shape the dough into a round, then place it in a lightly oiled bowl, cover and leave to rise in a warm place until doubled in size.

3 Knock back the dough on a lightly floured surface, then cut off one third of the dough. Shape both pieces of dough into plump balls and place each one on a baking sheet. Cover and leave to rise in a warm place until doubled in size.

4 Meanwhile, preheat the oven to 220ºC/425ºF/gas mark 7. Gently flatten each ball of dough and carefully place the smaller ball on top of the larger. Gently push the floured handle of a wooden spoon down through the centre of the dough to join both pieces together, then slightly enlarge the hole with your fingers. Leave to rest for 5–10 minutes.

5 Lightly brush the loaf with beaten egg and dust with a little flour. Using a very sharp knife, make slashes at regular intervals around the top of the bread and around the base. Bake the loaf for about 30–35 minutes, or until the bread is golden brown and sounds hollow when tapped underneath. Transfer to a wire rack to cool. Serve in slices.

Flowerpot bread

PREPARATION TIME *20 minutes, plus rising* **COOKING TIME** *35–40 minutes* **MAKES** *2 loaves*

450g (1lb) strong plain brown flour

1½ teaspoons salt

25g (1oz) butter, diced

2 teaspoons easy-blend dried yeast

1 teaspoon caster sugar

55g (2oz) barley flakes, plus extra for sprinkling

1–2 tablespoons chopped fresh mixed herbs

1 tablespoon malt extract

about 250ml (9fl oz) warm water

milk, for glazing

To make in a breadmachine: use quantities as listed in main recipe but amend following ingredients and use 315ml (10½fl oz) water, 2 teaspoons caster sugar, and use fast-action dried yeast. Add ingredients to breadmachine in order specified in your instruction book. Use Dough setting, then continue as above from Step 4 of main recipe.

1 You will need 2 tempered earthenware/terracotta flowerpots (about 14cm /5½in in diameter and 12cm/4½in high) to mould the bread. To temper (seal) the new perfectly clean pots, brush liberally with vegetable oil inside and out, then place in a hot oven (200°C/400°F/gas mark 6) for about 30 minutes. Allow them to cool, then repeat this procedure until the pots are impregnated with oil. They should now only need a little greasing before use. Do not wash them after use, simply wipe clean with kitchen paper.

2 Grease the flowerpots and set aside. Mix the flour and salt in a bowl and rub in the butter. Add the yeast, sugar, barley flakes and herbs. Mix in the malt extract and enough warm water to form a soft dough.

3 Turn the dough onto a floured surface and knead until smooth. Shape into a round, then place in a lightly oiled bowl, cover and leave to rise in a warm place until doubled in size.

4 Knock back the dough on a floured surface and divide in half. Shape and fit each piece of dough into a flowerpot – the dough should roughly half-fill the pot. Cover and leave to rise again for 45–60 minutes, or until the dough almost reaches the top of the flowerpots.

5 Meanwhile, preheat the oven to 200°C/400°F/gas mark 6. Brush the tops of the loaves with a little milk and sprinkle with extra barley flakes.

6 Bake for about 35–40 minutes, or until the bread is risen and sounds hollow when tapped underneath. Turn the loaves out and place on a wire rack to cool. Serve in slices.

Rye and caraway bread

PREPARATION TIME *20 minutes, plus rising* **COOKING TIME** *30–40 minutes* **MAKES** *1 loaf (serves 12–14)*

350g (12oz) rye flour

200g (7oz) strong plain white flour

2 teaspoons salt

25g (1oz) butter, diced

2 teaspoons easy-blend dried yeast

2 teaspoons caraway seeds

1 tablespoon black treacle

1 tablespoon malt extract

150ml (¼ pint) warm milk

about 150ml (¼ pint) warm water

wholemeal flour, for dusting (optional)

1 Grease or flour a baking sheet and set aside. Mix the rye and white flours and salt in a large bowl, then rub in the butter. Stir in the yeast and caraway seeds. Make a well in the centre, then add the black treacle, malt extract, milk and enough warm water, mixing to form a soft dough.

2 Turn the dough onto a lightly floured surface and knead until smooth and elastic. Shape the dough into a round, then place it in a lightly oiled bowl, cover and leave to rise in a warm place until doubled in size.

3 Knock back the dough on a lightly floured surface and shape into an oval. Place on the baking sheet, cover and leave to rise again until doubled in size.

4 Meanwhile, preheat the oven to 200°C/400°F/gas mark 6. Using a sharp knife, cut several slashes in the top of the dough, then dust with a little wholemeal flour, if desired.

5 Bake for 30–40 minutes, or until the loaf sounds hollow when tapped underneath. Transfer to a wire rack to cool. Serve in slices.

Sweet potato bread

PREPARATION TIME *35 minutes, plus rising* **COOKING TIME** *30–35 minutes*
MAKES *1 large loaf (serves 14–16)*

350g (12oz) sweet potatoes

500g (1lb 2oz) strong plain white flour

2 teaspoons salt

1 sachet (7g/¼oz) easy-blend dried yeast

1½ teaspoons caraway seeds, plus extra for sprinkling

a few turns of freshly ground black pepper

about 175ml (6fl oz) warm water

1 Grease or flour a baking sheet and set aside. Peel and dice the potatoes, then cook them in a saucepan of boiling water for about 15 minutes, or until tender. Drain well, mash thoroughly and set aside to cool.

2 Sift the flour and salt into a large bowl, then add the mashed potatoes, rubbing it loosely into the flour. Stir in the yeast, caraway seeds and black pepper, then make a well in the centre and add enough warm water, mixing to form a soft dough.

3 Turn the dough onto a lightly floured surface and knead until smooth and elastic. Shape the dough into a round, then place it in a lightly oiled bowl, cover and leave to rise in a warm place until doubled in size.

4 Knock back the dough on a lightly floured surface and shape into a large round or oval loaf. Place on the baking sheet, cover and leave to rise again for about 30 minutes, or until doubled in size.

5 Meanwhile, preheat the oven to 200°C/400°F/gas mark 6. Lightly brush the top of the loaf with water and sprinkle with caraway seeds. Using a sharp knife, slash the top of the loaf with 3–4 diagonal cuts to make a criss-cross effect.

6 Bake the loaf for 30–35 minutes, or until the bread is risen, golden brown and sounds hollow when tapped underneath. Transfer to a wire rack to cool. Serve in slices.

Spiced walnut bread

PREPARATION TIME *20 minutes, plus rising*   **COOKING TIME** *30–35 minutes*
MAKES *1 loaf (serves 10–12)*

350g (12oz) strong plain white flour

1½ teaspoons salt

225g (8oz) strong plain wholemeal flour

1 sachet (7g/¼oz) easy-blend dried yeast

1 teaspoon ground cinnamon

a pinch of ground cloves

about 300ml (½ pint) warm water

200g (7oz) walnut halves, roughly chopped

a little milk, for glazing

1 Grease or flour a baking sheet and set aside. Sift the white flour and salt into a large bowl, then stir in the wholemeal flour, yeast and ground spices. Make a well in the centre, then add enough warm water, mixing to form a soft dough.

2 Turn the dough onto a lightly floured surface and knead until smooth and elastic. Shape the dough into a round, then place it in a lightly oiled bowl, cover and leave to rise in a warm place until doubled in size.

3 Knock back the dough on a lightly floured surface, then gently knead in 140g (5oz) chopped walnuts until evenly distributed. Shape into a round or oval and place on the baking sheet. Cover and leave to rise again for about 45 minutes, or until doubled in size.

4 Meanwhile, preheat the oven to 220°C/425°F/gas mark 7. Lightly brush the top of the loaf with milk, then scatter the remaining walnuts over the top.

5 Bake the loaf for 10 minutes, then reduce the oven temperature to 190°C/375°F/gas mark 5 and bake for a further 20–25 minutes, or until the bread is risen, lightly browned and sounds hollow when tapped underneath. Transfer to a wire rack to cool. Serve in slices.

Variation Use pecan nuts instead of walnuts.

Cheese and poppyseed plait

PREPARATION TIME *30 minutes, plus rising* **COOKING TIME** *30–40 minutes* **MAKES** *1 loaf (serves 10)*

450g (1lb) strong plain white flour

1½ teaspoons salt

25g (1oz) butter, diced

1 sachet (7g/¼oz) easy-blend dried yeast

85g (3oz) mature Cheddar cheese, finely grated

2 teaspoons mustard powder

a few turns of freshly ground black pepper

about 300ml (½ pint) warm milk, plus extra for glazing

poppy seeds, for sprinkling

1 Grease or flour a baking sheet and set aside. Sift the flour and salt into a large bowl, then rub in the butter. Stir in the yeast, cheese, mustard powder and black pepper. Make a well in the centre, then add enough milk, mixing to form a soft dough.

2 Turn the dough onto a floured surface and knead until smooth. Shape into a round, then place in a lightly oiled bowl, cover and leave to rise in a warm place until doubled in size.

3 Knock back the dough on a lightly floured surface, then divide it in half. Roll each piece of dough into a long sausage or rope shape and place them side by side, pinching them together at one end to seal. Loosely plait the ropes of dough together, then pinch them together at the other end. Place the plait on the baking sheet. Cover and leave to rise again for about 30 minutes, or until doubled in size.

4 Meanwhile, preheat the oven to 190°C/375°F/gas mark 5. Brush the plait with a little milk and sprinkle with poppy seeds. Bake for 30–40 minutes, or until the bread is risen, golden brown and sounds hollow when tapped underneath. Cover the loaf loosely with foil towards the end of the cooking time if it is browning too much. Transfer to a wire rack to cool. Serve in slices.

To make in a breadmachine: use quantities as listed in main recipe but amend following ingredients and use 300ml (½ pint) milk, 1¼ teaspoons salt and 1½ teaspoons fast-action dried yeast, and add 1½ teaspoons caster sugar. Add ingredients to breadmachine in order specified in your instruction book. Use Dough setting for this recipe, then continue as above from Step 3 of main recipe.

French baguettes

PREPARATION TIME *35 minutes, plus rising* COOKING TIME *35–40 minutes*
MAKES *3 baguettes (each baguette serves 2–3)*

400g (14oz) strong plain white flour

115g (4oz) plain white flour

2½ teaspoons salt

1 sachet (7g/¼oz) easy-blend dried yeast

about 300ml (½ pint) warm water

1 teaspoon cornflour

To make in a breadmachine: use quantities as listed in main recipe but amend following ingredients and use 450g (1lb) strong plain white flour, omit the plain white flour, use 315ml (10½fl oz) water and 1½ teaspoons fast-action dried yeast. Use 1½ teaspoons salt in dough; use remaining salt as instructed in Step 5 of main recipe. Add ingredients to breadmachine in order specified in your instruction book. Use French Dough or Dough setting, then continue from Step 3 of main recipe.

1 Flour a large baking sheet; set aside. Sift the flours and 1½ teaspoons salt into a large bowl, then stir in the yeast. Add enough warm water, mixing to form a soft dough.
2 Turn the dough onto a floured surface and knead until smooth. Shape into a round, then place in an oiled bowl, cover and leave to rise in a warm place until doubled in size.
3 Knock back the dough on a lightly floured surface, then divide it into 3 equal portions; shape each portion into a roll or baton about 25cm (10in) in length.
4 Place between the folds of a pleated tea towel for support, cover and leave to rise again until doubled in size.
5 Meanwhile, preheat the oven to 200°C/400°F/gas mark 6. Place a roasting tin of water on the bottom shelf of the oven. Make the glaze. Blend the remaining salt and the cornflour with 1 tablespoon water. Pour 125ml (4fl oz) water into a small saucepan and stir in the cornflour mixture. Bring to the boil, stirring, then remove from the heat.
6 Roll the loaves onto the baking sheet; brush the baguettes with some of the salt solution. Using a sharp knife, cut several diagonal slashes in the top of each loaf at regular intervals. Bake the baguettes for 35–40 minutes, brushing the surfaces of the loaves with the salt solution every 10 minutes or so, until the baguettes are brown, crisp and sound hollow when tapped underneath. Transfer to a wire rack. Serve warm or cold.

Greek black olive bread

PREPARATION TIME *30 minutes, plus rising* COOKING TIME *30–35 minutes*
MAKES *1 loaf (serves 10–12)*

200g (7oz) whole black olives

500g (1lb 2oz) strong plain white flour, plus extra for dusting

1 teaspoon salt

2 teaspoons easy-blend dried yeast

5 tablespoons extra virgin olive oil

about 250ml (9fl oz) warm water

1 Grease or flour a baking sheet and set aside. Using a sharp knife, remove and discard the stones from the olives and chop the flesh, then set aside. Sift the flour and salt into a large bowl, then stir in the yeast. Make a well in the centre, then add half the chopped olives, the oil and enough warm water, mixing to form a soft dough.

2 Turn the dough onto a lightly floured surface and knead until smooth and elastic. Shape the dough into a round, then place it in a lightly oiled bowl, cover and leave to rise in a warm place until doubled in size.

3 Knock back the dough on a lightly floured surface, then roll out to form a rectangle about 35 x 25cm (14 x 10in). Sprinkle the surface of the dough evenly with the remaining chopped olives, then roll up the dough tightly like a Swiss roll, starting from a short side. Pinch the edges of each end of the roll together to seal.

4 Place the loaf, seam-side down, on the baking sheet. Using a sharp knife, cut a slash down the length of the centre of the loaf, if desired. Cover and leave to rise again for about 1 hour, or until doubled in size.

5 Meanwhile, preheat the oven to 220°C/425°F/gas mark 7. Dust the loaf with a little sifted flour. Bake for 10 minutes, then reduce the oven temperature to 190°C/375°F/gas mark 5 and bake for a further 20–25 minutes, or until the bread is risen, golden brown and sounds hollow when tapped underneath. Transfer to a wire rack. Serve warm or cold in slices.

Pesto whirl bread

PREPARATION TIME *25 minutes, plus rising* **COOKING TIME** *25–30 minute*
MAKES *2 loaves (each loaf serves 10–12)*

700g (1lb 9oz) strong plain white flour

2 teaspoons salt

1 teaspoon caster sugar

2 teaspoons easy-blend dried yeast

50ml (2fl oz) olive oil

about 400ml (14fl oz) warm water

6 tablespoons ready-made green pesto sauce

1 Grease two 900g (2lb) loaf tins and set aside. Sift the flour and salt into a large bowl, then stir in the sugar and yeast. Make a well in the centre, then add the oil and enough warm water, mixing to form a soft dough.

2 Turn the dough onto a lightly floured surface and knead until smooth and elastic. Shape the dough into a round, then place it in a lightly oiled bowl, cover and leave to rise in a warm place until doubled in size.

3 Knock back the dough on a lightly floured surface, then divide it in half. Roll or pat out each piece of dough to form a rectangle about 30 x 20cm (12 x 8in) in size.

4 Spread some pesto sauce evenly over each rectangle of dough, then roll up each one fairly tightly like a Swiss roll, starting from a short side. Re-shape slightly if necessary and place in the loaf tins. Cover and leave to rise again until doubled in size.

5 Meanwhile, preheat the oven to 220°C/425°F/gas mark 7. Bake the loaves for 25–30 minutes, or until risen and golden brown. Turn out and cool on a wire rack. Serve in slices on its own or spread with butter.

Variation *Use ready-made red pesto sauce in place of traditional green pesto sauce.*

Honey oatmeal bread

PREPARATION TIME *20 minutes, plus rising* **COOKING TIME** *30–35 minutes*
MAKES *1 loaf (serves 12–14)*

550g (1¼lb) strong plain brown flour

2 teaspoons salt

15g (½oz) butter, diced

115g (4oz) rolled oats, plus extra for sprinkling

2 teaspoons easy-blend dried yeast

150ml (¼ pint) warm milk, plus extra for glazing

2 tablespoons thick set honey

about 225ml (8fl oz) warm water

1 Grease or flour a baking sheet and set aside. Mix the flour and salt in a large bowl, then rub in the butter. Stir in the oats and yeast. Make a well in the centre, then add the milk, honey and enough warm water, mixing to form a soft dough.

2 Turn the dough onto a lightly floured surface and knead until smooth and elastic. Shape the dough into a round, then place it in a lightly oiled bowl, cover and leave to rise in a warm place until doubled in size.

3 Knock back the dough on a floured surface and shape into a round. Place on the baking sheet, cover and leave to rise again for about 30 minutes, or until doubled in size.

4 Meanwhile, preheat the oven to 230°C/450°F/gas mark 8. Using a sharp knife, slash the top of the loaf down the centre, brush with a little milk and sprinkle with oats.

5 Bake the loaf for 10 minutes, then reduce the oven temperature to 200°C/400°F/gas mark 6 and bake for a further 20–25 minutes, or until the bread is risen, lightly browned and sounds hollow when tapped underneath. Transfer to a wire rack to cool. Serve in slices.

Chocolate bread

PREPARATION TIME *30 minutes, plus rising* **COOKING TIME** *25 minutes* **MAKES** *1 loaf (serves 8–10)*

225g (8oz) strong plain white flour

1 tablespoon cocoa powder

½ teaspoon salt

25g (1oz) butter, diced

1½ teaspoons fast-action dried yeast

55g (2oz) caster sugar

1 egg, lightly beaten

about 125ml (4fl oz) warm milk

115g (4oz) milk or plain chocolate, roughly chopped

icing sugar, for dusting

1 Grease a 450g (1lb) loaf tin or a deep 15cm (6in) round cake tin and set aside. Sift the flour, cocoa powder and salt into a large bowl, then rub in the butter. Stir in the yeast and caster sugar. Make a well in the centre, then add the egg and enough milk, mixing to form a soft dough.

2 Turn the dough onto a lightly floured surface and knead until smooth and elastic. Knead the chocolate into the dough. Shape into an oblong or round, then place in the tin. Cover and leave to rise in a warm place until doubled in size (this may take 2–3 hours).

3 Meanwhile, preheat the oven to 200°C/400°F/gas mark 6. Using a sharp knife, slash the top of the loaf diagonally a couple of times, if desired.

4 Bake the loaf for about 25 minutes, or until the bread is cooked and sounds hollow when tapped underneath. Loosely cover the loaf with foil towards the end of the cooking time if the top is browning too quickly. Turn out and cool on a wire rack. Dust with sifted icing sugar and serve in slices.

Variation Use milk or plain chocolate chips in place of the chopped chocolate pieces.

Soft wholemeal rolls

PREPARATION TIME *25 minutes, plus rising* **COOKING TIME** *15–20 minutes* **MAKES** *8 rolls*

225g (8oz) strong plain wholemeal flour, plus extra for dusting

1 teaspoon salt

25g (1oz) butter, diced

1½ teaspoons easy-blend dried yeast

1 teaspoon caster sugar

about 150ml (¼ pint) warm milk

1 Grease or flour 2 baking sheets and set aside. Mix the flour and salt in a large bowl, then rub in the butter. Stir in the yeast and sugar. Make a well in the centre, then add enough milk, mixing to form a soft dough.

2 Turn the dough onto a lightly floured surface and knead until smooth and elastic. Shape the dough into a round, then place it in a lightly oiled bowl, cover and leave to rise in a warm place until doubled in size.

3 Knock back the dough on a lightly floured surface, then divide it into 8 equal portions. Roll each portion of dough into a round or oval, press each one down firmly with the heel of your hand and release.

4 Place the rolls on the baking sheets, spacing them well apart, cover and leave to rise again for 20–30 minutes, or until doubled in size.

5 Meanwhile, preheat the oven to 220°C/425°F/gas mark 7. Lightly dust the tops of the rolls with flour. Bake for 15–20 minutes, or until the rolls are lightly browned.

6 Transfer to a wire rack to cool and cover with a clean, dry tea towel to keep the crusts soft. Serve warm or cold.

Breakfast rolls

PREPARATION TIME *25 minutes, plus rising*   **COOKING TIME** *15–20 minutes*   **MAKES** *10–12 rolls*

450g (1lb) strong plain white flour, plus extra for dusting

1 teaspoon salt

1½ teaspoons easy-blend dried yeast

a pinch of caster sugar

25g (1oz) butter, diced

150ml (¼ pint) warm milk, plus extra for glazing

about 150ml (¼ pint) warm water

1 Grease or flour 2 baking sheets and set aside. Sift the flour and salt into a large bowl, stir in the yeast and sugar, then rub in the butter. Make a well in the centre, then add the milk and enough warm water, mixing to form a soft dough.

2 Turn the dough onto a lightly floured surface and knead until smooth and elastic. Shape the dough into a round, then place it in a lightly oiled bowl, cover and leave to rise in a warm place until doubled in size.

3 Knock back the dough on a lightly floured surface; divide it into 10 or 12 equal portions. Shape each portion into a round or oval and place on the baking sheets, spacing them well apart. Cover and leave to rise again for about 30 minutes or until doubled in size.

4 Meanwhile, preheat the oven to 200°C/400°F/gas mark 6. Lightly brush the rolls with milk and dust with flour. Bake for 15–20 minutes, or until lightly browned. Transfer to a wire rack to cool. Serve warm or cold.

To make in a breadmachine: use quantities as listed in main recipe but amend following ingredients and use 150ml (¼ pint) milk, 150ml (¼ pint) water, 1½ teaspoons salt, 1½ teaspoons fast-action dried yeast and 2 teaspoons caster sugar. Add ingredients to breadmachine in order specified in your instruction book. Use Dough setting for this recipe, then continue as above from Step 3 of main recipe.

Bagels

PREPARATION TIME *55 minutes, plus rising* **COOKING TIME** *15–20 minutes* **MAKES** *12 bagels*

225g (8oz) strong plain white flour

1½ teaspoons salt

225g (8oz) strong plain wholemeal flour

1 sachet (7g/¼oz) easy-blend dried yeast

1 tablespoon caster sugar

2 tablespoons sunflower oil

about 300ml (½ pint) warm water

1 tablespoon granulated sugar

milk, for glazing

poppy seeds, sesame seeds or caraway seeds, for sprinkling (optional)

1 Grease 2 baking sheets well and set aside. Sift the white flour and salt into a large bowl, then stir in the wholemeal flour, yeast and caster sugar. Make a well in the centre, then add the oil and enough warm water, mixing to form a soft dough.

2 Turn the dough onto a lightly floured surface and knead until smooth and elastic. Shape the dough into a round, then place it in a lightly oiled bowl, cover and leave to rise in a warm place until doubled in size.

3 Knock back the dough on a lightly floured surface, then divide it into 12 equal portions. Shape each piece of dough into a ball, then, using the floured handle of a wooden spoon, make a hole through the centre of each ball. Enlarge the holes by pulling the dough outwards slightly to form rings, making sure the holes are big enough (bearing in mind that the holes will close slightly when the dough is risen and poached). Place on the baking sheets, cover and leave to rise again for about 30 minutes, or until doubled in size.

4 Meanwhile, preheat the oven to 200ºC/400ºF/gas mark 6. Heat a large pan of water until it is simmering, then stir in the granulated sugar until dissolved. Carefully drop each bagel into the simmering water (3 or 4 at a time) and poach for about 3 minutes, turning once.

5 Remove the bagels from the water, drain well, then return the bagels to the baking sheets. Brush each one with a little milk and sprinkle the tops with seeds, if desired.

6 Bake the bagels for 15–20 minutes, or until golden brown. Transfer to a wire rack to cool. Cut in half to serve, warm or cold.

Golden cheddar twists

PREPARATION TIME *25 minutes, plus rising* **COOKING TIME** *15–20 minutes* **MAKES** *10 twists*

500g (1lb 2oz) packet white bread mix

115g (4oz) mature Cheddar cheese, finely grated

1 teaspoon mustard powder

a few turns of freshly ground black pepper

about 300ml (½ pint) warm water

beaten egg or milk, to glaze

1 Grease or flour 2 baking sheets and set aside. Place the bread mix in a bowl and stir in 85g (3oz) cheese, the mustard powder and black pepper. Add enough warm water (according to packet instructions), mixing to form a soft dough.

2 Turn the dough onto a lightly floured surface and knead until smooth and elastic. Divide the dough into 10 equal portions. Roll each piece of dough into a long sausage or rope shape, then gently tie each one loosely in a single knot, pulling the ends through.

3 Place on the baking sheets, spacing them well apart, brush with beaten egg or milk and sprinkle with the remaining grated cheese. Cover and leave to rise in a warm place for about 30 minutes, or until doubled in size.

4 Meanwhile, preheat the oven to 200°C/400°F/gas mark 6. Bake the twists for 15–20 minutes, or until risen and golden brown. Transfer to a wire rack. Serve warm or cold.

To make in a breadmachine: *use quantities as listed in main recipe but amend following ingredients and use 325ml (11fl oz) water (or according to packet mix). Use 85g (3oz) cheese in dough; use remaining cheese as instructed in Step 3 of main recipe. Add ingredients to breadmachine in order specified in your instruction book. Use Dough setting for this recipe, then continue as above from Step 2 of main recipe (knocking back rather than kneading dough, then divide and shape dough and continue as directed).*

Sesame breadsticks

PREPARATION TIME *35 minutes, plus rising*   **COOKING TIME** *15 minutes*   **MAKES** *25–30 breadsticks*

225g (8oz) white bread mix

2 tablespoons olive oil, plus extra for glazing

about 150ml (¼ pint) warm water

about 75g (2¾oz) sesame seeds, for coating

1 Grease or flour 2 baking sheets and set aside. Place the bread mix in a bowl, then add the oil and enough warm water, mixing to form a soft dough.

2 Turn the dough onto a lightly floured surface and knead until smooth and elastic. Roll out to form a large rectangle about 43 x 20cm (17 x 8in) in size and about 5mm (¼in) thick.

3 Cut the rectangle in half lengthways to make 2 long, narrow rectangles (each about 43 x 10cm/17 x 4in in size). Cut each rectangle crossways into strips about 2.5cm (1in) wide. Roll and stretch each strip of dough until it is about 25cm (10in) long.

4 Spread the sesame seeds out on a chopping board. Lightly brush each dough stick with oil, then roll in the sesame seeds as each one is made. Place on the baking sheets, then leave in a warm place for 10 minutes.

5 Meanwhile, preheat the oven to 200°C/400°F/gas mark 6. Bake the breadsticks for about 15 minutes, or until golden brown and crisp, turning them over halfway through the cooking time. Transfer to a wire rack to cool. Serve cold. Store in an airtight container.

Variation Add 1–2 teaspoons dried Italian herb seasoning to the bread mix, before adding the oil and water. Shape and bake as above.

Garlic bubble ring

PREPARATION TIME *25 minutes, plus rising* **COOKING TIME** *30–40 minutes* **SERVES** *12*

500g (1lb 2oz) packet white bread mix

about 325ml (11fl oz) warm water

100g (3½oz) butter, melted

1 egg, beaten

25g (1oz) fresh Parmesan cheese, grated

2 cloves garlic, crushed

½ teaspoon salt

1 teaspoon dried Italian herb seasoning

1 Grease a 23cm (9in) loose-bottomed springform tin fitted with a tube base, or a ring mould, and set aside. Place the bread mix in a large bowl and add enough warm water (according to packet instructions), mixing to form a soft dough.

2 Turn the dough onto a lightly floured surface and knead until smooth and elastic. Divide the dough into 12 equal portions and roll each piece into a ball.

3 Combine the melted butter, egg, Parmesan cheese, garlic, salt and dried herbs in a small bowl, mixing well. Dip the dough balls into the butter mixture, coating them liberally all over, then arrange the dough balls in a single layer in the tin. Drizzle over any remaining butter mixture. Cover and leave to rise in a warm place until doubled in size.

4 Preheat the oven to 190ºC/375ºF/gas mark 5. Bake the ring for 30–40 minutes, or until risen and golden brown. Turn onto a wire rack. Pull the rolls apart to serve, warm or cold.

To make in a breadmachine: *use quantities as listed in main recipe but amend following ingredients and use 325ml (11fl oz) water (or according to packet mix). Add ingredients to breadmachine in order specified in your instruction book. Use Dough setting, then continue as above from Step 2 of main recipe (knocking back rather than kneading dough, then divide and shape dough and continue as directed).*

Cherry and hazelnut twists

PREPARATION TIME *30 minutes, plus rising*   **COOKING TIME** *15–20 minutes*   **MAKES** *12 twists*

225g (8oz) strong plain white flour

½ teaspoon salt

25g (1oz) butter, diced

1½ teaspoons easy-blend dried yeast

25g (1oz) caster sugar

85g (3oz) dried cherries, halved

55g (2oz) toasted hazelnuts, finely chopped

1½ teaspoons ground cinnamon

1 egg, lightly beaten

about 100ml (3½fl oz) warm milk, plus extra for glazing

25g (1oz) sugar cubes, coarsely crushed

1 Grease or flour 2 baking sheets and set aside. Sift the flour and salt into a large bowl, then rub in the butter. Stir in the yeast, caster sugar, cherries, hazelnuts and cinnamon. Make a well in the centre, then add the egg and enough milk, mixing to form a soft dough.

2 Turn the dough onto a lightly floured surface and knead until smooth and elastic. Shape the dough into a round, then place it in a lightly oiled bowl, cover and leave to rise in a warm place until doubled in size.

3 Knock back the dough on a lightly floured surface, then divide it into 12 equal pieces. Roll each piece of dough into a long sausage or rope shape, about 20cm (8in) long, then gently tie each one into a single knot, pulling the ends through, and place on the baking sheets. Cover and leave to rise again for about 45 minutes, or until doubled in size.

4 Meanwhile, preheat the oven to 190°C/375°F/gas mark 5. Brush the twists with a little milk and sprinkle with crushed sugar cubes. Bake the twists for 15–20 minutes, or until risen and golden brown. Transfer to a wire rack to cool. Serve warm or cold.

Quick breads

Quick breads are
relatively easy to make compared to
other types of bread: ingredients are simply
mixed together and baked, without the need for
prolonged kneading or rising periods. Some quick
breads, such as teabreads that have been enriched
with butter, eggs or fruit, should keep well for
several days; others, such as scones and
muffins, are best served freshly baked
and warm from the oven.

Tomato and olive soda bread

PREPARATION TIME *20 minutes* **COOKING TIME** *30–40 minutes*
MAKES *1 loaf (serves 8)*

450g (1lb) plain white flour

1½ teaspoons bicarbonate of soda

1½ teaspoons cream of tartar

1 teaspoon salt

a few turns of freshly ground black pepper

2 teaspoons dried herbes de Provence

55g (2oz) butter, diced

85g (3oz) sun-dried tomatoes in oil, drained, patted dry & finely chopped

85g (3oz) pitted black olives, drained & finely chopped

about 300ml (½ pint) buttermilk

1 Preheat the oven to 200°C/400°F/gas mark 6. Grease or flour a baking sheet and set aside. Sift the flour, bicarbonate of soda and cream of tartar into a large bowl, then stir in the salt, pepper and dried herbs. Lightly rub in the butter until the mixture resembles breadcrumbs.

2 Stir in the chopped tomatoes and olives, mixing well. Make a well in the centre, then gradually add enough buttermilk, mixing to form a soft dough.

3 Turn the dough onto a floured surface and knead lightly, then shape into a 20cm (8in) round. Place on the baking sheet and, using a sharp knife, mark the round into 8 even wedges.

4 Bake the loaf for 30–40 minutes, or until risen and golden brown. Transfer to a wire rack to cool. Serve warm or cold cut into wedges.

Wheaten bread

PREPARATION TIME *20 minutes* **COOKING TIME** *50–60 minutes*
MAKES *1 large loaf (serves 14–16)*

225g (8oz) plain white flour

2 teaspoons salt

450g (1lb) plain wholemeal flour

1 tablespoon caster sugar

2 teaspoons bicarbonate of soda

25g (1oz) butter, diced

about 600ml (1 pint) buttermilk

(2 x 284ml cartons of buttermilk should be just about the correct amount)

1 Preheat the oven to 190°C/375°F/gas mark 5. Grease a deep 20cm (8in) round loose-bottomed cake tin or a baking sheet and set aside.

2 Sift the white flour and salt into a bowl, then stir in the wholemeal flour, sugar and bicarbonate of soda. Lightly rub the butter into the flour mixture, then stir in enough buttermilk, mixing to form a soft dough.

3 Shape the dough into a round, then place it in the tin or on the baking sheet.

4 Bake the loaf for 50–60 minutes, or until it is risen, deep golden brown and crusty on the surface and sounds hollow when tapped underneath. Turn out onto a wire rack to cool. Serve warm or cold in slices.

Onion, olive and chive bread

PREPARATION TIME *25 minutes*   **COOKING TIME** *35–40 minutes*
MAKES *1 loaf (serves 8–10)*

2 tablespoons olive oil

2 onions, finely chopped

500g (1lb 2oz) self-raising
white flour

1 teaspoon salt

a pinch of hot chilli powder

3–4 tablespoons chopped
fresh chives

85g (3oz) pitted green olives
(drained weight), finely
chopped

2 eggs

about 150ml (¼ pint) milk

1 Preheat the oven to 200°C/400°F/gas mark 6. Grease or flour
a baking sheet and set aside. Heat the oil in a frying pan, add
the onions and sauté over a medium heat for about 10 minutes,
or until softened. Remove the pan from the heat and set aside.
2 Sift the flour and salt into a large bowl, then stir in the chilli
powder, chives, olives and onions. Add the eggs, then stir in
enough milk, mixing to form a soft, but not sticky dough.
3 Gather the dough together using your hands, then turn it
onto a lightly floured surface and knead gently for 1–2 minutes.
Shape the dough into an oval or round and place on the baking
sheet. Using a sharp knife, score the top of the dough with
several diagonal slashes, if desired.
4 Bake the loaf for 35–40 minutes, or until risen and lightly
browned. Transfer to a wire rack to cool. Serve warm or cold
in slices.

Variation Use red onions in place of standard onions.

Celery and walnut loaf

PREPARATION TIME *25 minutes* **COOKING TIME** *45–60 minutes*
MAKES *1 loaf (serves 8–10)*

225g (8oz) self-raising
white flour

1 teaspoon baking powder

55g (2oz) butter, diced

2 sticks celery, finely chopped

55g (2oz) walnuts, finely
chopped

85g (3oz) mature Cheddar
cheese, finely grated

sea salt & freshly ground
black pepper

1 egg, beaten

about 4 tablespoons milk

1 Preheat the oven to 190°C/375°F/gas mark 5. Grease a 450g
(1lb) loaf tin or a baking sheet and set aside. Sift the flour and
baking powder into a bowl, then lightly rub in the butter until
the mixture resembles breadcrumbs.
2 Stir in the celery, walnuts, cheese and seasoning and mix well.
Add the egg and enough milk, mixing to form a soft, but not
sticky dough. Turn the dough onto a lightly floured surface and
knead gently until smooth.
3 Shape the dough into an oblong and place it in the tin, or
shape the dough into a round and place it on the baking sheet.
4 Bake the loaf for 45–60 minutes, or until risen and golden
brown. Turn out onto a wire rack to cool. Serve warm or cold in
slices, spread with butter.

*To make in a breadmachine: remove kneading blade from bread pan;
grease and line base and sides of pan. Follow main recipe as above, then
transfer mixture to prepared pan; level surface. Select Bake Only setting and
bake for 45–50 minutes or until loaf is cooked. Remove bread pan from
machine; leave to stand for 5 minutes. Turn loaf out onto wire rack to cool.*

Ham and spinach pinwheels

PREPARATION TIME *20 minutes* COOKING TIME *10–15 minutes*
MAKES *about 14 pinwheels*

225g (8oz) self-raising white flour

1 teaspoon baking powder

a pinch of salt

55g (2oz) butter, diced

about 150ml (¼ pint) milk

1 tablespoon Dijon mustard

85g (3oz) cooked lean ham slices (smoked or unsmoked), diced

25g (1oz) fresh baby spinach leaves, shredded

85g (3oz) Gruyère cheese, grated

1 Preheat the oven to 220°C/425°F/gas mark 7. Grease 2 baking sheets and set aside. Sift the flour, baking powder and salt into a bowl, then lightly rub in the butter until the mixture resembles breadcrumbs. Make a well in the centre, then stir in enough milk, mixing to form a soft dough.

2 Turn the dough onto a lightly floured surface and knead gently. Roll out to form a rectangle approximately 30 x 23cm (12 x 9in). Spread the mustard evenly over the dough.

3 Combine the ham, spinach and cheese and sprinkle this mixture evenly over the dough. Starting on a long side, roll up the dough fairly tightly like a Swiss roll. Trim the edges off each end of the roll and discard the trimmings, then cut the roll into about 14 even slices.

4 Place the slices on the baking sheets, leaving a little space between each one. Bake for 10–15 minutes, or until risen and golden brown. Transfer to a wire rack to cool and serve warm or cold.

Variations Use ready-made green or red pesto sauce in place of mustard. Use fresh Parmesan cheese in place of Gruyère.

Hot cheese triangles

PREPARATION TIME *20 minutes* **COOKING TIME** *10 minutes*
MAKES *8–10 triangles*

115g (4oz) self-raising white flour

a pinch of salt

1 teaspoon baking powder

115g (4oz) self-raising wholemeal flour

1 teaspoon mustard powder

25g (1oz) butter, diced

115g (4oz) Red Leicester cheese, finely grated

about 150ml (¼ pint) milk, plus extra for glazing

1 Preheat the oven to 220°C/425°F/gas mark 7. Grease or flour a large baking sheet and set aside. Sift the white flour, salt and baking powder into a bowl, then stir in the wholemeal flour and mustard powder.
2 Lightly rub in the butter until the mixture resembles breadcrumbs, then stir in 85g (3oz) cheese. Make a well in the centre, then stir in enough milk, mixing to form a soft dough.
3 Turn the dough onto a lightly floured surface, knead gently, then roll or pat out to about 2.5cm (1in) thickness. Cut into even triangles. Place the triangles on the baking sheet, leaving a little space between each one. Brush the tops with milk, then sprinkle over the remaining cheese.
4 Bake the scone triangles for about 10 minutes, or until well-risen and golden brown. Transfer to a wire rack to cool. Serve hot, warm or cold.

Variation *Use Emmental or Cheddar cheese in place of Red Leicester.*

Pesto whirls

PREPARATION TIME *20 minutes* **COOKING TIME** *12–15 minutes*
MAKES *about 20 whirls*

225g (8oz) self-raising white flour

1 teaspoon baking powder

1 teaspoon mustard powder

a pinch of salt

a few turns of freshly ground black pepper

55g (2oz) butter, diced

1 egg, beaten

3–4 tablespoons milk

5 tablespoons ready-made green pesto sauce

85g (3oz) fresh Parmesan cheese, finely grated

1 Preheat the oven to 200°C/400°F/gas mark 6. Grease 2 baking sheets and set aside. Sift the flour, baking powder and mustard powder into a bowl. Stir in the salt and pepper, then lightly rub in the butter until the mixture resembles breadcrumbs.
2 Make a well in the centre, then add the egg and enough milk, mixing to form a soft dough. Turn the dough onto a lightly floured surface and knead gently.
3 Roll out the dough to form a rectangle approximately 35 x 25cm (14 x 10in). Spread the pesto sauce evenly over the dough, almost to the edges, then sprinkle the Parmesan cheese evenly over the top. From a long side, roll up the dough fairly tightly like a Swiss roll, then cut into 1.5cm (⅝in) slices using a sharp knife.
4 Place the whirls on the baking sheets, leaving a little space between each one. Bake for 12–15 minutes, or until golden brown. Transfer to a wire rack to cool. Serve warm or cold.

Variation Once cut and placed on the baking sheets, sprinkle the whirls with extra grated cheese or sesame seeds before baking, if desired.

Wholemeal cheese scones

PREPARATION TIME *20 minutes* COOKING TIME *15–20 minutes*
MAKES *6–8 scones*

225g (8oz) plain wholemeal flour

1 tablespoon baking powder

a pinch of salt

a good pinch of cayenne pepper

40g (1½oz) butter, diced

140g (5oz) mature Cheddar cheese, finely grated

about 150ml (¼ pint) milk, plus extra for glazing

1 Preheat the oven to 200°C/400°F/gas mark 6. Grease a baking sheet and set aside. Mix the flour, baking powder, salt and cayenne pepper in a bowl, then lightly rub in the butter until the mixture resembles breadcrumbs. Stir in 115g (4oz) of the cheese, then add enough milk, mixing to form a soft dough.

2 Knead the dough gently, then roll or pat out on a lightly floured surface until about 2–2.5cm (¾–1in) thick. Cut out 6–7.5cm (2½–3in) rounds using a plain or fluted cutter. Place the scones on the baking sheet, leaving a little space between each one.

3 Brush the tops with milk and sprinkle with the remaining cheese. Bake for 15–20 minutes, or until risen and golden brown. Transfer to a wire rack to cool. Serve warm or cold.

Mini Parmesan scones

PREPARATION TIME *20 minutes*   COOKING TIME *8–10 minutes*
MAKES *about 32 mini scones*

225g (8oz) self-raising
white flour

a pinch of salt

25g (1oz) butter, diced

115g (4oz) fresh Parmesan
cheese, finely grated

1 egg, beaten

about 100ml (3½fl oz) milk,
plus extra for glazing

1 tablespoon sesame seeds
(optional)

1 Preheat the oven to 220°C/425°F/gas mark 7. Grease or flour 2 baking sheets and set aside. Sift the flour and salt into a bowl, then lightly rub in the butter until the mixture resembles breadcrumbs. Stir in 85g (3oz) cheese, then add the egg and enough milk, mixing to form a soft dough.
2 Turn the dough onto a lightly floured surface, knead gently, then roll or pat out lightly until about 1cm (½in) thick. Cut into rounds or squares using a 2.5cm (1in) cutter or sharp knife. Place on the baking sheets, leaving a little space between each one.
3 Brush the tops with milk, then mix together the remaining cheese and sesame seeds, if using, and sprinkle over the top.
4 Bake the scones for 8–10 minutes, or until well risen and golden brown. Transfer to a wire rack to cool. Serve warm or cold.

Apple and cinnamon scone round

PREPARATION TIME *20 minutes* **COOKING TIME** *25–30 minutes*
SERVES *8*

115g (4oz) self-raising white flour

a pinch of salt

1 teaspoon baking powder

115g (4oz) self-raising wholemeal flour

40g (1½oz) butter, diced

55g (2oz) light soft brown sugar

1 teaspoon ground cinnamon

1 medium cooking apple (about 300g/10½oz in weight), peeled, cored & coarsely grated

3–4 tablespoons milk, plus extra for glazing

1 tablespoon demerara sugar

1 Preheat the oven to 200°C/400°F/gas mark 6. Grease or flour a baking sheet and set aside. Sift the white flour, salt and baking powder into a bowl, then stir in the wholemeal flour. Lightly rub in the butter until the mixture resembles breadcrumbs.

2 Stir in the soft brown sugar and cinnamon, then add the grated apple and mix well. Stir in enough milk to form a soft, but not sticky dough.

3 Turn the dough onto a floured surface, knead lightly, then shape into an 18cm (7in) round.

4 Place the scone round on the baking sheet, brush the top with milk and sprinkle with the demerara sugar. Using a sharp knife, mark the top of the scone round into 8 even wedges, cutting deeply into the dough.

5 Bake the scone round for 25–30 minutes, or until risen and golden brown. Transfer to a wire rack to cool. Break into wedges and serve warm or cold.

Variation *Use ground mixed spice or ginger in place of cinnamon.*

Fresh strawberry scones

PREPARATION TIME *15 minutes*   **COOKING TIME** *8–10 minutes*
MAKES *12 scones*

225g (8oz) self-raising wholemeal flour

1 teaspoon baking powder

a pinch of salt

55g (2oz) butter, diced

25g (1oz) caster sugar

100g (3½oz) fresh strawberries, chopped

about 125ml (4fl oz) milk, plus extra for glazing

strawberry jam & whipped cream or crème fraîche, to serve

1 Preheat the oven to 220°C/425°F/gas mark 7. Grease or flour a baking sheet and set aside. Put the flour, baking powder and salt in a large bowl and stir to mix, then lightly rub in the butter until the mixture resembles breadcrumbs. Stir in the sugar and strawberries, then add enough milk, mixing to form a soft dough.

2 Turn the dough onto a lightly floured surface, knead gently, then lightly roll or pat out until about 2cm (¾in) thick. Cut out 12 rounds using a 5cm (2in) pastry cutter, and place on the baking sheet, leaving a little space between each one. Brush the tops with milk to glaze.

3 Bake the scones for 8–10 minutes, or until well risen and golden brown. Transfer to a wire rack to cool. Split in half to serve, spread with butter, if desired, and top with jam and cream or crème fraîche. Serve warm or cold.

Variations Use 115g (4oz) self-raising white flour in place of half of the wholemeal flour, if desired. To give these scones a warm, spicy flavour, add 1 teaspoon ground cinnamon with the flour at the start of the recipe.

Blueberry wedges

PREPARATION TIME *15 minutes* **COOKING TIME** *20–25 minutes*
SERVES *8*

225g (8oz) self-raising wholemeal flour

a pinch of salt

1 teaspoon baking powder

1 teaspoon ground cinnamon

55g (2oz) butter, diced

55g (2oz) caster sugar

115g (4oz) fresh blueberries, washed & dried

4 tablespoons soured cream

about 125ml (4fl oz) milk

1 Preheat the oven to 200°C/400°F/gas mark 6. Grease a baking sheet and set aside. Mix the flour, salt, baking powder and cinnamon in a bowl, then lightly rub in the butter until the mixture resembles breadcrumbs. Stir in the sugar and blueberries, then add the soured cream and enough milk, mixing to form a fairly soft dough.

2 Knead the dough briefly on a lightly floured surface, then shape the dough into a 20cm (8in) round. Place the scone round on the baking sheet. Using a sharp knife, mark the top of the scone round into 8 even wedges, cutting fairly deeply into the dough.

3 Bake the scone round for 20–25 minutes, or until risen and lightly browned. Transfer to a wire rack to cool. Cut or break the scone round into wedges and serve warm or cold.

Variation Use ground mixed spice in place of cinnamon.

Malted fruit loaf

PREPARATION TIME *20 minutes* **COOKING TIME** *40 minutes*
MAKES *1 loaf (serves 10–12)*

225g (8oz) self-raising white flour

1 teaspoon bicarbonate of soda

1 teaspoon ground mixed spice

3 tablespoons malt extract

2 tablespoons golden syrup

125ml (4fl oz) milk

1 egg, beaten

140g (5oz) sultanas

2 tablespoons clear honey, to glaze

1 Preheat the oven to 180°C/350°F/gas mark 4. Grease and line a 900g (2lb) loaf tin and set aside. Sift the flour, bicarbonate of soda and mixed spice into a bowl. Set aside.

2 Place the malt extract, syrup and milk in a saucepan and heat gently until melted and blended, stirring occasionally. Remove the pan from the heat and cool slightly, then mix in the egg.

3 Make a well in the centre of the dry ingredients, then add the melted mixture, mixing well with a wooden spoon. Fold in the sultanas. Transfer to the loaf tin and level the surface.

4 Bake the loaf for about 40 minutes, or until risen and browned. Cover loosely with foil towards the end of the cooking time if the top is browning too quickly.

5 Cool slightly in the tin, then turn out onto a wire rack. While the loaf is still warm, brush it twice with honey to glaze. Leave to cool and serve warm or cold in slices.

Fruit and spice teabread

PREPARATION TIME *20 minutes* **COOKING TIME** *1 hour*
MAKES *1 loaf (serves 10–12)*

225g (8oz) self-raising white flour

½ teaspoon bicarbonate of soda

1 tablespoon ground mixed spice

115g (4oz) light soft brown sugar

115g (4oz) sultanas

115g (4oz) raisins

115g (4oz) currants

115g (4oz) ready-to-eat dried apricots, finely chopped

2 eggs

150ml (¼ pint) milk

1 Preheat the oven to 180°C/350°F/gas mark 4. Grease a 900g (2lb) loaf tin and set aside. Sift the flour, bicarbonate of soda and mixed spice into a bowl.

2 Add the sugar and dried fruit and mix well. Beat the eggs and milk together and add to the fruit mixture. Beat until thoroughly mixed. Turn the mixture into the loaf tin and level the surface.

3 Bake the loaf for about 1 hour, or until risen, golden brown and firm to the touch.

4 Remove the teabread from the oven and allow to cool in the tin for a few minutes, then turn out onto a wire rack. Serve warm or cold in slices.

To make in a breadmachine: remove kneading blade from bread pan; grease and line base and sides of pan. Follow main recipe as above, then transfer mixture to prepared pan; level surface. Select Bake Only setting and bake for 60–70 minutes or until teabread is cooked. Remove bread pan from machine; leave to stand for 5 minutes. Turn teabread out of bread pan onto wire rack to cool.

Golden gingerbread

PREPARATION TIME *20 minutes, plus cooling* **COOKING TIME** *1–1¼ hours*
MAKES *1 loaf (serves 8–10)*

115g (4oz) light soft brown sugar

85g (3oz) butter

175g (6oz) golden syrup

225g (8oz) plain white flour

a pinch of salt

1 teaspoon baking powder

2 teaspoons ground ginger

1 egg, beaten

150ml (¼ pint) milk

1 Preheat the oven to 170°C/325°F/gas mark 3. Grease and line a 900g (2lb) loaf tin and set aside. Place the sugar, butter and syrup in a saucepan and heat gently until melted and blended, stirring. Remove the pan from the heat and cool slightly.

2 Sift the flour, salt, baking powder and ginger into a bowl and make a well in the centre. Mix together the egg and milk and pour into the centre of the dry ingredients together with the melted mixture. Beat together using a wooden spoon until smooth and thoroughly mixed. Pour the mixture into the loaf tin.

3 Bake the gingerbread for 1–1¼ hours, or until risen and lightly browned and a fine skewer inserted in the centre comes out clean.

4 Remove from the oven and allow to cool in the tin for a few minutes, then turn out onto a wire rack. Serve warm or cold in slices.

To make in a breadmachine: remove kneading blade from bread pan; grease and line base and sides of pan. Follow main recipe as above, then transfer mixture to prepared pan; level surface. Select Bake Only setting and bake for 60–70 minutes or until gingerbread is cooked. Remove bread pan from machine; leave to stand for 5 minutes. Turn gingerbread out onto wire rack to cool.

Chocolate banana bread

PREPARATION TIME *20 minutes*   **COOKING TIME** *1–1¼ hours*
MAKES *1 loaf (serves 10–12)*

115g (4oz) butter, softened

115g (4oz) light soft
brown sugar

115g (4oz) thick set honey

2 eggs, beaten

225g (8oz) self-raising
white flour

½ teaspoon baking powder

25g (1oz) cocoa powder

2 ripe bananas, peeled &
mashed with a little lemon
juice (total weight of bananas
including skins = about
300g/10½oz)

about 1 tablespoon milk

sifted icing sugar, for dusting

1 Preheat the oven to 180°C/350°F/gas mark 4. Grease and
line a 900g (2lb) loaf tin and set aside. Cream the butter, soft
brown sugar and honey together in a bowl until light and
fluffy. Gradually beat in the eggs. Sift the flour, baking powder
and cocoa powder into the bowl, then fold into the creamed
mixture, mixing well.

2 Fold in the mashed bananas and enough milk, mixing to form
a fairly soft consistency. Transfer the mixture to the loaf tin and
level the surface.

3 Bake in the oven for 1–1¼ hours, or until risen and firm to
the touch and a fine skewer inserted in the centre comes out
clean. Cover loosely with foil for the last 30 minutes or so of the
cooking time if the top is browning too quickly.

4 Remove the loaf from the oven and allow to cool in the tin for
a few minutes, then turn out onto a wire rack. Dust with sifted
icing sugar and serve warm or cold in slices.

Iced raisin loaf

PREPARATION TIME *20 minutes, plus soaking overnight* **COOKING TIME** *1¼ hours*
MAKES *1 loaf (serves 10–12)*

225g (8oz) raisins

115g (4oz) sultanas

300ml (½ pint) strong hot tea, strained

225g (8oz) light soft brown sugar

300g (10½oz) self-raising white flour

1½ teaspoons ground mixed spice

1 egg, beaten

175g (6oz) icing sugar, sifted

about 5–6 teaspoons orange juice

1 Place the raisins and sultanas in a large bowl, pour over the hot tea and stir to mix. Cover and leave to soak overnight.
2 The next day, preheat the oven to 170°C/325°F/gas mark 3. Grease and line a 900g (2lb) loaf tin and set aside. Stir the brown sugar into the dried fruit mixture, then sift in the flour and mixed spice. Add the egg and stir with a wooden spoon until thoroughly mixed.
3 Turn the mixture into the loaf tin and level the surface. Bake for about 1¼ hours, or until risen and firm to the touch – a fine skewer inserted in the centre should come out clean.
4 Remove the loaf from the oven and allow to cool in the tin for a few minutes, then turn out onto a wire rack and leave to cool completely.
5 Combine the icing sugar with enough orange juice to make a thick icing. Spread this icing evenly over the top of the cake. Leave to set. Serve in slices.

Double chocolate-chip muffins

PREPARATION TIME *25 minutes* **COOKING TIME** *20 minutes*
MAKES *12 muffins*

225g (8oz) self-raising white flour

2 teaspoons baking powder

a pinch of salt

40g (1½oz) cocoa powder, sifted

115g (4oz) light soft brown sugar

225ml (8fl oz) milk

115g (4oz) natural yoghurt

1 egg, lightly beaten

1 teaspoon vanilla essence

55g (2oz) butter, melted

175g (6oz) milk or plain chocolate, roughly chopped into small chunks

1 Preheat the oven to 200°C/400°F/gas mark 6. Grease each cup of a 12-cup muffin tin or line each cup with a paper muffin case. Set aside. Sift the flour, baking powder, salt and cocoa powder into a large bowl, then stir in the sugar.

2 Combine the milk, yoghurt, egg and vanilla essence, then stir this into the flour mixture together with the melted butter, mixing well. Fold in the chopped chocolate. Divide the mixture evenly between the muffin cups, filling each one about three-quarters full.

3 Bake the muffins for about 20 minutes, or until risen and firm to the touch. Transfer to a wire rack to cool. Serve warm or cold.

Variation *Use milk, plain or white chocolate chips in place of chopped chocolate pieces.*

Raisin and orange muffins

PREPARATION TIME *20 minutes* **COOKING TIME** *15–20 minutes*
MAKES *9 large or 12 medium-sized muffins*

115g (4oz) plain wholemeal flour

85g (3oz) plain white flour

1 tablespoon baking powder

a pinch of salt

55g (2oz) butter, melted

55g (2oz) caster sugar

1 egg, beaten

200ml (7fl oz) milk

finely grated zest of 1 orange

115g (4oz) raisins

1 Preheat the oven to 200°C/400°F/gas mark 6. Grease 9 or 12 cups of a 12-cup muffin tin or line each cup with a paper muffin case and set aside. Reserve 25g (1oz) wholemeal flour and set aside. Put the remaining wholemeal flour in a bowl, then sift the white flour, baking powder and salt into the bowl and stir to mix.
2 Mix together the melted butter, sugar, egg, milk and orange zest. Pour the egg mixture over the dry ingredients, then fold the ingredients gently together – just enough to combine the mixture. The mixture should look quite lumpy; over-mixing will result in heavy muffins. Toss the raisins in the remaining flour, then fold gently into the muffin mixture.
3 Spoon the mixture into the muffin cups, dividing it evenly between each one.
4 Bake the muffins for 15–20 minutes, or until well risen and golden brown. Transfer to a wire rack to cool. Serve warm or cold.

Variations Use lemon zest in place of orange zest. Use sultanas or dried blueberries in place of raisins.

Cheesy bacon muffins

PREPARATION TIME *20 minutes*   **COOKING TIME** *20 minutes*
MAKES *12 muffins*

300g (10½oz) self-raising white flour

½ teaspoon baking powder

1 teaspoon paprika

a pinch of salt

85g (3oz) butter, diced

6 rashers cold cooked lean smoked back bacon (about 140g/5oz), chopped

175g (6oz) medium or mature Cheddar cheese, grated

1 egg, beaten

250ml (9fl oz) milk

1 Preheat the oven to 200°C/400°F/gas mark 6. Grease each cup of a 12-cup muffin tin or line each cup with a paper muffin case. Set aside. Sift the flour, baking powder, paprika and salt into a large bowl, then lightly rub in the butter.
2 Stir in the bacon and cheese, then add the egg and milk, stirring gently to mix well.
3 Spoon the mixture into the muffin cups, dividing it evenly between each one.
4 Bake the muffins for about 20 minutes, or until well risen, golden brown and firm to the touch. Transfer to a wire rack to cool. Serve warm or cold.

Variations Just before baking, sprinkle each muffin with a little extra grated cheese, if desired. Use Emmental, Gruyère or Red Leicester cheese in place of Cheddar.

Mini maple pecan muffins

PREPARATION TIME *30 minutes* **COOKING TIME** *10 minutes*
MAKES *about 48 mini muffins*

225g (8oz) plain white flour

1 tablespoon baking powder

a pinch of salt

55g (2oz) light soft
brown sugar

55g (2oz) butter, melted

3 tablespoons maple syrup

150ml (¼ pint) milk

2 eggs, beaten

115g (4oz) pecan nuts,
finely chopped

sifted icing sugar, to decorate
(optional)

1 Preheat the oven to 200°C/400°F/gas mark 6. Line two 24-cup mini muffin tins with paper cases or lay out about 48 paper mini muffin cases on 2 baking sheets. Set aside. Sift the flour, baking powder and salt into a bowl, then stir in the soft brown sugar.
2 Combine the melted butter, maple syrup, milk and eggs in a separate bowl. Make a well in the centre of the dry ingredients and pour in the egg mixture. Gently fold the ingredients together, just enough to combine the mixture. The mixture should look quite lumpy; over-mixing will result in heavy muffins.
3 Gently fold in the pecan nuts, then spoon the mixture into the muffin cases, filling each one about two-thirds full.
4 Bake the muffins for about 10 minutes, or until well risen and golden brown. Transfer to a wire rack to cool. Dust with sifted icing sugar just before serving, if desired. Serve warm or cold.

Variations Use chopped walnuts in place of pecan nuts. Use golden syrup or clear honey in place of maple syrup.

Flat breads

From Indian naan breads
to Italian focaccias, flat breads – whether
leavened or unleavened – vary in texture,
flavour and shape. They may be crisp or doughy,
plain or rich, and most of them are quick and easy
to prepare and cook. Many flat breads make an ideal
accompaniment to a main meal and are great for
dipping or mopping up sauces. Here we include
a variety of popular flat bread recipes
from around the world.

Naan bread

PREPARATION TIME *20 minutes, plus rising* **COOKING TIME** *10–12 minutes*
MAKES *4 good-sized naan bread*

300g (10½oz) strong plain
white flour

1 teaspoon salt

1½ teaspoons easy-blend
 dried yeast

4 tablespoons natural yoghurt
(at room temperature)

1 tablespoon sunflower oil

about 125ml (4fl oz)
warm milk

about 3 tablespoons melted
ghee or butter, for brushing

1 Sift the flour and salt into a large bowl, then stir in the yeast.
Make a well in the centre, then add the yoghurt, oil and enough
milk, mixing to form a soft dough.
2 Turn the dough onto a floured surface and knead until
smooth. Shape into a round, then place in a lightly oiled bowl,
cover and leave to rise in a warm place until doubled in size.
3 Knock back the dough on a lightly floured surface, then divide
into 4 equal portions. Roll out each piece of dough to form a flat
oval or teardrop shape, about 5mm (¼in) thick and 23cm (9in)
long. Cover and leave for 15 minutes.
4 Preheat the oven to 230°C/450°F/gas mark 8. Put 2 baking
sheets in the oven to heat. Place the naan breads on the hot
baking sheets and brush with melted ghee or butter.
5 Bake for 10–12 minutes, or until puffed up. Wrap in a clean
tea towel and serve warm.

To make in a breadmachine: *use quantities as listed in main recipe but
amend following ingredients and use 120ml (4fl oz) milk and 1 teaspoon
fast-action dried yeast, and add 1½ teaspoons caster sugar. Add ingredients to breadmachine in order specified in your instruction book. Use Basic
Dough or Pizza Dough setting for this recipe, then continue as above from
Step 3 of main recipe.*

Puris (Pooris)

PREPARATION TIME *20 minutes, plus resting* **COOKING TIME** *20–25 minutes* **MAKES** *20 puris*

115g (4oz) plain white flour

1 teaspoon salt

125g (4½oz) plain wholemeal flour

2 tablespoons vegetable oil, plus extra for deep-frying

about 100ml (3½fl oz) warm water

1 Sift the white flour and salt into a bowl, then stir in the wholemeal flour. Make a well in the centre, then add the 2 tablespoons oil, and enough warm water, mixing with your hands to form quite a stiff dough.

2 Turn the dough onto a lightly floured surface and knead for about 5 minutes, or until smooth and elastic. Shape the dough into a round, then place it in a clean bowl, cover with a damp cloth and leave to rest for 1 hour.

3 Divide the dough into about 20 equal portions. On a lightly floured surface, roll each portion of dough into a thin round about 10–12cm (4–4½in) in diameter and 2–3mm (1⁄16–1⁄8in) thick.

4 Heat some oil (a depth of about 8cm/3¼in) in a deep, heavy-based pan until hot. Add one round of dough to the oil and deep-fry for about 30 seconds, or until the puri puffs up and is golden brown underneath. Using a wooden spoon or spatula, turn the puri over and deep-fry for about 30 seconds, or until golden brown all over.

5 Remove from the oil using a slotted spoon or fish slice, drain on kitchen paper and keep warm. Repeat with the remaining rounds of dough. Serve hot.

Variation *Use buckwheat, rye or chapati flour in place of wholemeal flour.*

Moroccan flat breads

PREPARATION TIME *25 minutes, plus rising*   COOKING TIME *15–20 minutes*
MAKES *4 flat breads (each flat bread serves 1)*

280g (10oz) strong plain white flour

¼ teaspoon salt

1 teaspoon fennel seeds

1 teaspoon easy-blend dried yeast

2 teaspoons clear honey

about 175ml (6fl oz) warm milk

beaten egg, to glaze

1 Grease or flour 2 baking sheets and set aside. Sift the flour and salt into a large bowl, then stir in the fennel seeds and yeast. Make a well in the centre, then add the honey and enough milk, mixing to form a soft dough.
2 Turn the dough onto a lightly floured surface and knead until smooth and elastic. Shape the dough into a round, then place it in a lightly oiled bowl, cover and leave to rise in a warm place until doubled in size.
3 Knock back the dough on a lightly floured surface and divide it into 4 equal portions. Roll each portion into a round about 9cm (3½in) in diameter, and about 2cm (¾in) thick.
4 Place on the baking sheets, then using a sharp knife or scissors, cut twelve 1cm (½in) deep slashes all around the edge of each dough round at regular intervals. Cover and leave in a warm place for 20 minutes.
5 Preheat the oven to 220°C/425°F/gas mark 7. Brush the tops of the dough rounds with beaten egg, then bake for 15–20 minutes, or until the breads are risen slightly and golden brown. Transfer to a wire rack to cool. Serve whole or cut into quarters.

To make in a breadmachine: use quantities as listed in main recipe but amend following ingredients and use 175ml (6fl oz) milk, 1 teaspoon salt and use fast-action dried yeast. Add ingredients to breadmachine in order specified in your instruction book. Use Basic Dough or Pizza Dough setting for this recipe, then continue as above from Step 3 of main recipe.

Pitta bread

PREPARATION TIME *25 minutes, plus rising* **COOKING TIME** *10 minutes*
MAKES *8 pitta bread*

350g (12oz) strong plain
white flour

1 teaspoon salt

1½ teaspoons easy-blend
dried yeast

1 teaspoon caster sugar

1 tablespoon olive oil

about 225ml (8fl oz)
warm water

1 Sift the flour and salt into a large bowl, then stir in the yeast and sugar. Make a well in the centre, then add the oil and enough warm water, mixing to form a soft dough.

2 Turn the dough onto a lightly floured surface and knead until smooth and elastic. Shape the dough into a round, then place it in a lightly oiled bowl, cover and leave to rise in a warm place until doubled in size.

3 Knock back the dough on a lightly floured surface, then divide it into 8 equal portions. Roll out each piece of dough to form a flat oval, about 3–5mm (⅛–¼in) thick and about 14–15cm (5½–6in) in length. Lay the dough ovals on a floured tea towel, cover and leave to rise at normal room temperature for about 30 minutes.

4 Meanwhile, preheat the oven to 230°C/450°F/gas mark 8. Put 3 baking sheets in the oven to heat. Place the pitta breads on the hot baking sheets and bake for about 10 minutes, or until puffed up and golden brown.

5 Serve warm or wrap in a clean tea towel and leave to cool on a wire rack, then re-heat under a grill when required. To serve, split open and stuff with your favourite filling.

To make in a breadmachine: use ingredient quantities as listed in main recipe but amend following ingredients and use 225ml (8fl oz) water, 1½ teaspoons salt and 1 teaspoon fast-action dried yeast. Add ingredients to breadmachine in order specified in your instruction book. Use Basic Dough or Pizza Dough setting for this recipe, then continue as above from Step 3 of main recipe.

Blue cheese and bacon quiche

PREPARATION TIME *1 hour, 10 minutes, plus rising* **COOKING TIME** *35 minutes*
MAKES *2 quiches (each quiche serves 6–8)*

FOR THE DOUGH

500g (1lb 2oz) strong plain white flour

1 teaspoon salt

3 teaspoons fast-action dried yeast

3 tablespoons olive oil

2 eggs, beaten

about 200ml (7fl oz) warm milk

fresh herb sprigs, to garnish

FOR THE FILLING

55g (2oz) butter

450g (1lb) smoked back bacon, diced

4 onions, thinly sliced

225g (8oz) blue cheese, such as Stilton or Roquefort, crumbled

8 eggs

500ml (17fl oz) single cream

sea salt & freshly ground black pepper

1 Make the dough. Sift the flour and salt into a large bowl, then stir in the yeast. Make a well in the centre, then add the oil, eggs and enough milk, mixing to form a soft dough.

2 Turn the dough onto a lightly floured surface and knead until smooth and elastic. Divide in half, then roll out each piece and use each to line a 28cm (11in) fluted tart tin. Cover and leave to rise in a warm place for 30 minutes.

3 Gently press back the risen dough in the tins to re-shape it, if necessary. Meanwhile, preheat the oven to 190°C/375°F/gas mark 5 and prepare the filling. Melt the butter in a frying pan, add the bacon and sauté for 5 minutes, or until just cooked. Remove to a plate and keep warm. Add the onions to the pan and sauté for 8 minutes, or until softened.

4 Place half the bacon in the flan cases and top with the onions, cheese and remaining bacon. Beat the eggs, cream and seasoning together, then pour over the bacon and cheese.

5 Bake each quiche (one at a time) in the oven for about 35 minutes, or until the case is cooked and the filling is lightly set and golden. Garnish with herb sprigs. Serve warm.

Pancetta, pepper and olive pizza

PREPARATION TIME *45 minutes, plus rising*   **COOKING TIME** *20–25 minutes*
MAKES *2 pizzas (each pizza serves 4–6)*

FOR THE PIZZA DOUGH

450g (1lb) strong plain white flour

1 teaspoon salt

1½ teaspoons easy-blend dried yeast

2 tablespoons olive oil

about 250ml (9fl oz) warm water

FOR THE TOPPING

2 tablespoons olive oil

2 cloves garlic, crushed

225g (8oz) smoked pancetta, diced

2 large red peppers, seeded & sliced

400g (14oz) can chopped tomatoes with herbs, drained

2 tablespoons tomato purée

sea salt & freshly ground black pepper

115–175g (4–6oz) whole black olives

115g (4oz) Parmesan cheese, grated

1 Grease or flour 2 baking sheets. Sift the flour and salt into a large bowl, then stir in the yeast. Make a well in the centre, then add the oil and enough warm water, mixing to form a soft dough.
2 Turn the dough onto a floured surface and knead until smooth. Shape into a round, then place in a lightly oiled bowl, cover and leave to rise in a warm place until doubled in size.
3 Prepare the topping. Heat the oil in a frying pan, add the garlic and sauté for 30 seconds. Add the pancetta and stir-fry until it releases its fat and browns. Remove from the pan and set aside. Add the peppers to the pan and sauté for 7 minutes. Remove the pan from the heat and add the pancetta to the peppers.
4 Knock back the dough on a lightly floured surface, then divide it in half. Roll out each piece thinly to form a 30cm (12in) round. Transfer each round to a baking sheet. Mix together the chopped tomatoes, tomato purée and seasoning. Spread this mixture over the bases to within 1cm (½in) of the edge. Spoon the pepper and pancetta mixture evenly over the tomatoes, then scatter the olives over the top. Sprinkle with the Parmesan.
5 Meanwhile, preheat the oven to 220°C/425°F/gas mark 7. Bake each pizza (one at a time) for 20–25 minutes, or until the base is crisp and the topping is golden. Serve warm.

To make in a breadmachine: use quantities as listed in main recipe but amend following ingredients and use 280ml (9½fl oz) water, use fast-action dried yeast, and add 2 teaspoons caster sugar. Add ingredients to breadmachine in order specified in your instruction book. Use Basic Dough or Pizza Dough setting for this recipe, then continue as above from Step 3.

Sun-dried tomato & olive focaccia

PREPARATION TIME *30 minutes, plus rising* **COOKING TIME** *20–25 minutes*
MAKES *1 loaf (serves 6)*

450g (1lb) strong plain white flour

1 teaspoon salt

2 teaspoons easy-blend dried yeast

55g (2oz) sun-dried tomatoes in oil, drained & chopped

55g (2oz) pitted black olives, chopped

3 tablespoons olive oil, plus extra for drizzling

about 250ml (9fl oz) warm water

coarse sea salt, for sprinkling

1 Grease or flour a baking sheet and set aside. Sift the flour and salt into a large bowl, then stir in the yeast. Stir in the tomatoes and olives. Make a well in the centre, then add the 3 tablespoons oil and enough warm water, mixing to form a soft dough.

2 Turn the dough onto a lightly floured surface and knead until smooth and elastic. Shape the dough into a round, then place it in a lightly oiled bowl, cover and leave to rise in a warm place until doubled in size.

3 Knock back the dough on a lightly floured surface, then roll out to form a flat oval about 2.5cm (1in) thick. Place the dough on the baking sheet, cover and leave to rise again until doubled in size.

4 Meanwhile, preheat the oven to 200°C/400°F/gas mark 6. Using your fingertips, make deep dimples all over the surface of the dough. Drizzle with oil and sprinkle with sea salt. Bake for 20–25 minutes, or until cooked and golden. Transfer to a wire rack to cool. Serve warm or cold in chunks or slices.

Drop scones

PREPARATION TIME *10 minutes* **COOKING TIME** *20 minutes* **MAKES** *10–12 drop scones*

115g (4oz) self-raising white flour

25g (1oz) caster sugar

1 egg, beaten

150ml (¼ pint) milk

sunflower oil, for greasing

1 Sift the flour into a bowl, then stir in the sugar. Make a well in the centre and stir in the egg, then gradually stir in the milk, mixing to make a smooth, thick, creamy batter.

2 Grease a griddle or large, heavy-based frying pan until hot. Cook the mixture in batches and drop spoonfuls of the mixture onto the hot griddle. Cook over a moderate heat for 2–3 minutes until the top surface of the scones is covered with bubbles and the underside is golden. Turn over using a palette knife and cook for a further 2–3 minutes until golden on the other side.

3 Remove from the griddle and wrap in a warm, clean tea towel. Repeat with the remaining batter, until all the batter is used up. Serve the drop scones warm, spread with butter, jam or honey.

Variation Once the underside of the scones is just set and almost cooked, sprinkle each one with a few currants, then turn them over and cook the other side.

English muffins

PREPARATION TIME *25 minutes, plus rising* **COOKING TIME** *35 minutes* **MAKES** *8–10 muffins*

500g (1lb 2oz) strong plain white flour

1½ teaspoons salt

1½ teaspoons easy-blend dried yeast

1 teaspoon caster sugar

55g (2oz) butter, melted

150ml (¼ pint) warm milk

about 150ml (¼ pint) warm water

sunflower oil, for greasing

To make in breadmachine: use quantities as listed in main recipe but amend following ingredients and use 450g (1lb) strong plain white flour, 140ml (4½fl oz) milk, 125ml (4fl oz) water and use fast-action dried yeast. Add ingredients to breadmachine in order specified in your instruction book. Use Dough setting for this recipe, then continue as above from Step 3 of main recipe.

1 Generously flour a large baking sheet and set aside. Sift the flour and salt into a large bowl, then stir in the yeast and sugar. Make a well in the centre, then add the melted butter, milk and enough warm water, mixing to form a soft dough.
2 Turn the dough onto a lightly floured surface and knead until smooth and elastic. Shape the dough into a round, then place it in a lightly oiled bowl, cover and leave to rise in a warm place until doubled in size.
3 Knock back the dough on a lightly floured surface and divide it into 8–10 equal portions. Shape each portion into a round with straight sides, each about 1–2cm (½–¾in) thick. Place on the baking sheet, cover and leave to rise again for about 30–40 minutes, or until springy to the touch.
4 Brush a griddle or large, heavy-based frying pan with a little oil and heat until warm. Carefully transfer 3–4 muffins onto the griddle and cook in batches over a moderate heat for 8–10 minutes, or until golden brown underneath. Turn them over and cook the other side for about 8 minutes, or until golden brown.
5 Remove the muffins from the pan and wrap them in a clean tea towel, if serving warm. Otherwise transfer them to a wire rack to cool. Cook the remaining muffins.
6 To serve, split the muffins open and serve with butter. If serving from cold, toast the muffins on both sides, then split and spread with butter.

Rye crispbreads

PREPARATION TIME *25 minutes, plus rising* **COOKING TIME** *20 minutes* **MAKES** *about 20 crispbreads*

350g (12oz) strong plain white flour

2 teaspoons salt

175g (6oz) rye flour

25g (1oz) butter, diced

2 teaspoons easy-blend dried yeast

1 tablespoon fennel seeds

1 tablespoon black treacle

about 300ml (½ pint) warm water

1 Grease 3 baking sheets and set aside. Sift the white flour and salt into a bowl, then stir in the rye flour. Rub in the butter, then stir in the yeast and fennel seeds. Make a well in the centre, then add the black treacle and enough warm water, mixing to form a firm dough.

2 Turn the dough onto a lightly floured surface and knead until smooth, firm and elastic. Shape the dough into a round, then place it in a lightly oiled bowl, cover and leave to rise in a warm place until doubled in size.

3 Knock back the dough on a lightly floured surface, then divide into 20 equal portions. Roll each portion into a small round about 10cm (4in) in diameter and about 3mm (⅛in) thick.

4 Using a fork, prick each round of dough all over, then place them on the baking sheets. Cover and leave to rise again for about 30–45 minutes, or until slightly risen.

5 Meanwhile, preheat the oven to 190°C/375°F/gas mark 5. Bake the crispbreads for about 20 minutes, or until slightly risen, lightly browned and crisp. Transfer to a wire rack to cool. Serve cold.

Pretzels

PREPARATION TIME *30 minutes, plus rising* COOKING TIME *20 minutes* MAKES *about 8 pretzels*

400g (14oz) strong plain white flour

1 teaspoon fine salt

1 teaspoon caster sugar

1½ teaspoons easy-blend dried yeast

15g (½oz) butter, melted

125ml (4fl oz) warm milk

about 125ml (4fl oz) warm water

beaten egg, to glaze

coarse sea salt or caraway seeds, for sprinkling

1 Grease or flour 2 baking sheets and set aside. Sift the flour and fine salt into a large bowl, then stir in the sugar and yeast. Make a well in the centre, then add the melted butter, milk and enough warm water, mixing to form a soft dough.

2 Turn the dough onto a lightly floured surface and knead until smooth and elastic. Shape the dough into a round, then place it in a lightly oiled bowl, cover and leave to rise in a warm place until doubled in size.

3 Knock back the dough on a lightly floured surface, then divide it into 8 equal portions. Roll each piece of dough into a long thin rope, about 40cm (16in) in length. Bend each rope into a horseshoe shape, then lift up the ends and cross them over. Press the ends lightly onto the curve of the horseshoe to give a knotted effect.

4 Preheat the oven to 200°C/400°F/gas mark 6. Place the pretzels on the baking sheets and brush with beaten egg, then sprinkle them with coarse sea salt or caraway seeds.

5 Bake the pretzels for about 20 minutes, or until they are slightly risen and golden brown – they will be slightly crispy on the outside and soft and doughy on the inside. Transfer to a wire rack to cool. Serve cold.

Variations *Replace 115g (4oz) of the white flour with rye flour. Sprinkle the pretzels with sesame seeds in place of coarse salt or caraway seeds.*

Breadmachine recipes

Breadmachines take
the hard work out of breadmaking and
allow you to be creative and produce a wide
range of delicious sweet and savoury breads with
very little effort. They also enable you to create shaped
breads and rolls, such as plaits and knots, enriched
doughs such as croissants, and speciality loaves such
as baguettes, by using the Dough Only setting
and then baking them in an oven in the
conventional way.

Basic white bread

PREPARATION TIME *10 minutes* **COOKING TIME** *varies according to breadmachine*
MAKES *1 medium loaf (serves 10)*

350ml (12fl oz) water

500g (1lb 2oz) strong plain white flour

1 tablespoon skimmed milk powder

1½ teaspoons salt

2 teaspoons granulated sugar

25g (1oz) butter, diced

1 teaspoon fast-action dried yeast

1 Please note, bread machines vary, so add the ingredients to the bread pan in the order specified in your instruction book (if this differs from the instructions given here).

2 Pour the water into the bread machine pan. Sprinkle over the flour, covering the water completely. Sprinkle the milk powder over the flour. Add the salt, sugar and butter, placing them in separate corners of the bread pan. Make a small indent in the centre of the flour and add the yeast.

3 Close the lid, set the machine to the programme recommended in the manual (usually Basic White/Normal setting), select size of loaf and type of crust and press Start.

4 Once the baking cycle has finished, remove the bread pan from the machine and turn out the loaf onto a wire rack to cool. Serve in slices.

Basic brown bread

PREPARATION TIME *10 minutes* **COOKING TIME** *varies according to breadmachine*
MAKES *1 medium loaf (serves 10)*

350ml (12fl oz) water

250g (9oz) strong plain wholemeal flour

250g (9oz) strong plain white flour

1 tablespoon skimmed milk powder

1½ teaspoons salt

2 teaspoons granulated sugar

25g (1oz) butter, diced

1 teaspoon fast-action dried yeast

1 Please note, bread machines vary, so add the ingredients to the bread pan in the order specified in your instruction book (if this differs from the instructions given here).

2 Pour the water into the bread machine pan. Sprinkle over each type of flour in turn, ensuring that the water is completely covered. Sprinkle the milk powder over the flour. Add the salt, sugar and butter, placing them in separate corners of the bread pan. Make a small indent in the centre of the flour and add the yeast.

3 Close the lid, set the machine to the programme recommended in the manual (usually Basic White/Normal or Wholewheat setting), select size of loaf and type of crust and press Start.

4 Once the baking cycle has finished, remove the bread pan from the machine and turn out the loaf onto a wire rack to cool. Serve in slices.

Six-seed bread

PREPARATION TIME *10 minutes* **COOKING TIME** *varies according to breadmachine*
MAKES *1 medium loaf (serves 10)*

300ml (½ pint) water

2 tablespoons sunflower oil

225g (8oz) strong plain white flour

225g (8oz) strong granary flour

1 tablespoon skimmed milk powder

1½ teaspoons salt

2 teaspoons granulated sugar

1 teaspoon fast-action dried yeast

2 tablespoons sunflower seeds

1 tablespoon pumpkin seeds

2 teaspoons EACH of sesame seeds & poppy seeds

1 teaspoon EACH of caraway seeds & cumin or fennel seeds

1 Please note, bread machines vary, so add the ingredients to the bread pan in the order specified in your instruction book (if this differs from the instructions given here).

2 Pour the water into the bread machine pan, then add the oil. Sprinkle over each type of flour in turn, covering the water completely. Sprinkle the milk powder over the flours. Add the salt and sugar, placing them in separate corners of the bread pan. Make a small indent in the centre of the flour and add the yeast.

3 Close the lid, set the machine to the programme recommended in the manual (usually Basic White/Normal setting, with Raisin setting or similar, if available), select size of loaf and type of crust and press Start. Combine the seeds. Add the mixed seeds when the machine makes a sound (beeps) to add extra ingredients during the kneading cycle (or 5 minutes before the end of the kneading cycle).

4 Once the baking cycle has finished, remove the bread pan from the machine and turn out the loaf onto a wire rack to cool. Serve in slices.

Variation *Packets of prepared mixed seeds suitable for breadmaking are available. Use 5 tablespoons ready-mixed seeds in place of seeds listed above.*

Rosemary ciabatta rolls

PREPARATION TIME *20 minutes, plus mixing & kneading time in breadmachine, plus rising*
COOKING TIME *20 minutes* **MAKES** *about 10 good-sized rolls*

350ml (12fl oz) water

2 tablespoons olive oil

500g (1lb 2oz) strong plain white flour, plus extra for dusting

1 teaspoon salt

1 teaspoon granulated sugar

1 teaspoon fast-action dried yeast

1 tablespoon finely chopped fresh rosemary

milk, for glazing

1 Please note, bread machines vary, so add the ingredients to the bread pan in the order specified in your instruction book (if this differs from the instructions given here).

2 Pour the water into the bread machine pan, then add the oil. Sprinkle over the flour, covering the water completely. Add the salt and sugar, placing them in separate corners of the bread pan. Make a small indent in the centre of the flour and add the yeast. Close the lid, set the machine to the Dough setting and press Start.

3 Meanwhile, grease or flour 2 baking sheets and set aside. When the dough cycle has finished, remove the dough from the machine, knock it back on a lightly floured surface, then knead the chopped rosemary evenly into the dough.

4 Divide the dough into about 10 equal portions. Roll and shape each piece into a round or oval, then flatten slightly. Place on the baking sheets, spacing them well apart. Cover and leave to rise in a warm place for about 30 minute, or until doubled in size.

5 Preheat the oven to 200ºC/400ºF/gas mark 6. Brush the tops of the rolls with milk and dust with flour. Bake in the oven for about 20 minutes, or until they are golden brown and sound hollow when tapped underneath. Transfer to a wire rack to cool. Serve warm.

Sun-dried tomato bread

PREPARATION TIME *10 minutes* **COOKING TIME** *varies according to breadmachine*
MAKES *1 medium loaf (serves 8–10)*

300ml (½ pint) water

1 tablespoon oil from a jar of sun-dried tomatoes

450g (1lb) strong plain white flour

55g (2oz) fresh Parmesan cheese, finely grated

1½ teaspoons salt

2 teaspoons caster sugar

1 teaspoon fast-action dried yeast

55g (2oz) sun-dried tomatoes in oil (drained weight), patted dry & chopped

1 Please note, bread machines vary, so add the ingredients to the bread pan in the order specified in your instruction book (if this differs from the instructions given here).
2 Pour the water into the bread machine pan, then add the oil. Sprinkle over the flour, ensuring that the water is completely covered. Sprinkle over the Parmesan cheese. Add the salt and sugar, placing them in separate corners of the bread pan. Make a small indent in the centre of the flour and add the yeast.
3 Close the lid, set the machine to the programme recommended in the manual (usually Basic White/Normal setting, with Raisin setting or similar, if available), select size of loaf and type of crust and press Start.
4 Add the sun-dried tomatoes when the machine makes a sound (beeps) to add extra ingredients during the kneading cycle (or 5 minutes before the end of the kneading cycle).
5 Once the baking cycle has finished, remove the bread pan from the machine and turn out the loaf onto a wire rack to cool. Serve in slices.

Sesame bagels

PREPARATION TIME *10 minutes, plus mixing & kneading time in breadmachine, plus 10 minutes to shape bagels, plus rising* **COOKING TIME** *20 minutes* **MAKES** *12 bagels*

275ml (9½ fl oz) water

2 tablespoons sunflower oil

450g (1lb) strong plain white flour

1½ teaspoons salt

1 tablespoon caster sugar

1 sachet (7g/¼oz) fast-action dried yeast

1 tablespoon malt extract

milk or water, for glazing

about 2 tablespoons sesame seeds, for sprinkling

1 Please note, bread machines vary, so add the ingredients to the bread pan in the order specified in your instruction book (if this differs from the instructions given here).

2 Pour the water into the bread machine pan, then add the oil. Sprinkle over the flour, covering the water completely. Add the salt and sugar, placing them in separate corners of the bread pan. Make a small indent in the centre of the flour and add the yeast. Close the lid, set the machine to the Dough setting and press Start.

3 Meanwhile, grease 2 baking sheets. When the dough cycle has finished, remove the dough from the machine, knock it back on a lightly floured surface, then divide it into 12 equal portions.

4 Shape each piece of dough into a ball, then, using the floured handle of a wooden spoon, make a hole through the centre of each ball. Enlarge the holes by pulling the dough outwards slightly to form rings, making sure the holes are big enough (bearing in mind they will close slightly when the dough is risen and poached). Place on the baking sheets, cover and leave to rise in a warm place for about 30 minutes, or until doubled in size.

5 Meanwhile, preheat the oven to 200ºC/400ºF/gas mark 6. Heat a large pan of water until it is simmering, then stir in the malt extract until dissolved. Carefully drop each bagel into the simmering water (three or four at a time) and poach for about 3 minutes, turning once. Remove the bagels from the water using a slotted spoon, drain well, then return the bagels to the baking sheets.

6 Brush each one with a little milk or water and sprinkle the tops with sesame seeds. Bake the bagels in the oven for about 20 minutes, or until cooked and golden brown. Transfer to a wire rack to cool. Cut in half to serve.

Poppyseed knots

PREPARATION TIME *20 minutes, plus mixing & kneading in breadmachine, plus rising*
COOKING TIME *15–20 minutes* **MAKES** *10 knots*

warm water, to mix
(according to bread mix
packet instructions)

500g (1lb 2oz) packet white
bread mix

beaten egg or milk, to glaze

poppy seeds, for sprinkling

1 Please note, bread machines vary, so add the ingredients to the bread pan in the order specified in your instruction book (if this differs from the instructions given here).

2 Pour the correct amount of water (according to bread mix packet instructions) into the bread machine pan. Sprinkle over the bread mix, covering the water completely. Close the lid, set the machine to the Dough setting and press Start.

3 Meanwhile, grease or flour 2 baking sheets and set aside. When the dough cycle has finished, remove the dough from the machine, knock it back on a lightly floured surface, then divide it into 10 equal portions. Roll each piece of dough into a long sausage or rope shape, then gently tie each one loosely in a single knot, pulling the ends through.

4 Place on the baking sheets, spacing them well apart, brush with beaten egg or milk, and sprinkle with poppy seeds. Cover and leave to rise in a warm place for about 30 minutes, or until doubled in size.

5 Meanwhile, preheat the oven to 200ºC/400ºF/gas mark 6. Bake the knots in the oven for 15–20 minutes, or until risen and golden brown. Transfer to a wire rack to cool. Serve warm or cold.

Herby polenta bread

PREPARATION TIME *10 minutes* **COOKING TIME** *varies according to breadmachine*
MAKES *1 medium loaf (serves 10)*

300ml (½ pint) water

3 tablespoons clear honey

3 tablespoons chopped fresh mixed herbs such as flat-leaf parsley, chives & basil

55g (2oz) polenta

350g (12oz) strong plain wholemeal flour

115g (4oz) strong plain white flour

1½ teaspoons salt

25g (1oz) butter, diced

1½ teaspoons fast-action dried yeast

1 Please note, bread machines vary, so add the ingredients to the bread pan in the order specified in your instruction book (if this differs from the instructions given here).
2 Pour the water into the bread machine pan, then add the honey. Sprinkle over the chopped herbs and polenta, then sprinkle over each of the flours in turn, covering the water completely. Add the salt and butter, placing them in separate corners of the bread pan. Make a small indent in the centre of the flour and add the yeast.
3 Close the lid, set the machine to the programme recommended in the manual (usually Wholewheat setting), select size of loaf and type of crust and press Start.
4 Once the baking cycle has finished, remove the bread pan from the machine and turn out the loaf onto a wire rack to cool. Serve in slices.

Variation *Use maple syrup in place of honey.*

Lemon blueberry loaf

PREPARATION TIME *15 minutes* **COOKING TIME** *1–1¼ hours*
MAKES *1 loaf (serves 10)*

225g (8oz) self-raising white flour

115g (4oz) butter, diced

115g (4oz) caster sugar

40g (1½oz) ground almonds or ground hazelnuts

finely grated zest & juice of 1 lemon

2 eggs, beaten

4 tablespoons milk

200g (7oz) fresh blueberries, rinsed & dried

55g (2oz) icing sugar, sifted

1 Remove the kneading blade from the bread pan and grease and line the base and sides of the pan. Sift the flour into a bowl, then lightly rub in the butter. Stir in the caster sugar, nuts and lemon zest, then beat in the eggs and milk, mixing well. Fold in the blueberries.

2 Spoon the mixture into the pan and level the surface. Place the bread pan in position in the machine and close the lid. Select the Bake Only setting and enter 60 minutes on the timer. Press Start.

3 After baking, a fine skewer inserted in the centre of the loaf should come out clean. If the loaf requires further baking, select the same programme as before and enter a further 10–15 minutes on the timer, or until the loaf is risen and cooked.

4 Remove the bread pan from the machine using oven gloves, then leave to stand for 10 minutes, before turning the loaf out of the pan onto a wire rack to cool.

5 Combine the icing sugar with 1–2 teaspoons lemon juice to give a fairly thin glacé icing. Drizzle the icing over the cold loaf. Serve in slices.

Variation Spread the top of the cold cooked loaf with lemon buttercream icing in place of glacé icing, if preferred.

Marbled chocolate teabread

PREPARATION TIME *25 minutes*   COOKING TIME *1 hour*   MAKES *1 loaf (serves 10)*

175g (6oz) butter, softened

175g (6oz) light soft brown sugar

3 eggs, beaten

225g (8oz) plain white flour

2½ teaspoons baking powder

2 ripe bananas, peeled & mashed with a little lemon juice (total weight of bananas including skins = about 300g/10½oz)

25g (1oz) cocoa powder

2 teaspoons milk

½ teaspoon ground ginger

sifted icing sugar & cocoa powder, for dusting

1 Remove the kneading blade from the bread pan and grease and line the base and sides of the pan. Cream the butter and brown sugar together in a bowl. Gradually beat in the eggs. Sift the flour and baking powder into the bowl; fold in, mixing well. Fold in the bananas.

2 Place half the teabread mixture in a separate bowl and sift the cocoa powder into this bowl. Add the milk and fold the ingredients together. Stir the ground ginger into the plain banana mixture in the other bowl.

3 Place alternate spoonfuls of each teabread mixture into the pan, then gently swirl a sharp knife or skewer through the mixture to create a marbled effect.

4 Place the bread pan in position in the machine and close the lid. Select the Bake Only setting and enter 55 minutes on the timer. Press Start. After baking, a fine skewer inserted in the centre of the teabread should come out clean. If the teabread requires further baking, select the same programme as before and enter a further 5–10 minutes on the timer, or until the teabread is cooked.

5 Remove the bread pan from the machine using oven gloves, then leave to stand for 10 minutes, before turning the teabread out of the pan onto a wire rack. Dust with sifted icing sugar and cocoa powder and serve warm or cold in slices.

Gluten-free breads

For those with a sensitivity to
gluten, this chapter will be an invaluable
source of imaginative hand-made and
breadmachine recipes for you to enjoy. Gluten-free
breads, by the very nature of their ingredients, tend to
be slightly different in texture and flavour to ordinary
breads, but are just as delicious. They have a slightly
more crumbly, closer, but light texture, and
are enjoyed at their best when served
warm and freshly baked.

Cheesy onion cornbread

PREPARATION TIME *35 minutes* **COOKING TIME** *30 minutes*
MAKES *1 loaf (serves 8–10)*

1 tablespoon sunflower oil

1 onion, thinly sliced

175g (6oz) gluten-free maize (corn) meal

85g (3oz) rice flour

25g (1oz) soya flour

1 tablespoon gluten-free baking powder

1 teaspoon caster sugar

1 teaspoon salt

115g (4oz) mature Cheddar cheese, coarsely grated

200ml (7fl oz) warm milk

2 eggs, lightly beaten

40g (1½oz) butter, melted

1 Preheat the oven to 190°C/375°F/gas mark 5. Grease a 900g (2lb) loaf tin and set aside. Heat the oil in a frying pan, add the onion and cook gently for 10–15 minutes, or until softened, stirring occasionally. Remove the pan from the heat and set aside to cool.

2 Place the maize (corn) meal, rice flour, soya flour, baking powder, sugar and salt in a bowl and mix well. Stir in the cheese. In a small bowl, beat together the milk, eggs and melted butter, then add to the flour mixture, stirring to mix well.

3 Reserve about 1 tablespoon of the cooled, cooked onions. Stir the remaining onions into the bread mixture. Transfer the mixture to the loaf tin and level the surface. Sprinkle the reserved onions evenly over the top.

4 Bake for about 30 minutes, or until the loaf is risen and golden brown. Turn out and cool on a wire rack. Serve warm or cold in slices.

Variations Use 4–6 shallots in place of onion. Use Gruyère or Emmental cheese in place of Cheddar.

Fresh herb bread

PREPARATION TIME *15 minutes* **COOKING TIME** *varies according to breadmachine*
MAKES *1 medium loaf (serves 10–12)*

400g (14oz) gluten-free white bread flour

55g (2oz) gram (chickpea) flour

275ml (9½fl oz) water

2 eggs, beaten

4 tablespoons olive oil

4 tablespoons chopped fresh mixed herbs (parsley, basil, oregano, chives)

55g (2oz) fresh Parmesan cheese, finely grated

1 tablespoon caster sugar

1½ teaspoons salt

2½ teaspoons fast-action dried yeast

1 Please note, bread machines vary, so add the ingredients to the bread pan in the order specified in your instruction book (if this differs from the instructions given here). Mix the flours together and set aside. Place the water in a bowl, add the eggs, oil and chopped herbs and whisk together until well mixed.

2 Pour the water mixture into the bread machine pan. Sprinkle over the Parmesan cheese, then the flours, covering the liquid completely. Sprinkle the sugar evenly over the flour, then add the salt. Make a small indent in the centre of the flour and add the yeast.

3 Close the lid, set the machine to the programme recommended in the manual (usually Rapid Bake setting gives the best results), select size of loaf and type of crust and press Start. A couple of minutes after mixing has begun, lift the lid of the machine briefly and scrape down the sides of the pan with a plastic spatula to ensure even mixing. Close the lid once again.

4 Once the baking cycle has finished, remove the bread pan from the machine and turn out the loaf onto a wire rack to cool. Serve in slices.

Soya bread

PREPARATION TIME *20 minutes, plus rising* **COOKING TIME** *25–30 minutes*
MAKES *1 loaf (serves 12–14)*

350g (12oz) brown rice flour

55g (2oz) soya flour

1 teaspoon salt

55g (2oz) butter, diced

55g (2oz) mature Cheddar cheese, grated

1 sachet (7g/¼oz) fast-action dried yeast

1 teaspoon light soft brown sugar

1 egg, beaten

250ml (9fl oz) warm milk

150ml (¼ pint) warm water

1 Grease a 1.1kg (2½lb) loaf tin and set aside. Place the rice flour, soya flour and salt in a bowl and stir to mix. Lightly rub in the butter, then stir in the cheese, yeast and sugar. Make a well in the centre, then add the egg, milk and water and beat together until thoroughly mixed to form a smooth, thick consistency.
2 Transfer the mixture to the loaf tin and level the surface. Cover and leave in a warm place for about 45 minutes, or until the mixture has risen to the top of the tin.
3 Meanwhile, preheat the oven to 200°C/400°F/gas mark 6. Bake the loaf for 25–30 minutes, or until lightly browned. Remove from the oven, turn out and cool on a wire rack. Serve warm or cold in slices.

Red onion and rosemary pizza

PREPARATION TIME *25 minutes* **COOKING TIME** *25–30 minutes*
MAKES *1 pizza (serves 4–6)*

2 tablespoons olive oil

2 red onions, thinly sliced

1 clove garlic, thinly sliced

1 red or yellow pepper, seeded & sliced

115g (4oz) gluten-free maize (corn) meal

55g (2oz) potato flour

55g (2oz) soya flour

1 teaspoon gluten-free baking powder

½ teaspoon salt

55g (2oz) butter, diced

about 7 tablespoons milk

4 plum tomatoes, skinned, seeded & chopped

2–3 teaspoons chopped fresh rosemary

sea salt & freshly ground black pepper

140g (5oz) mozzarella cheese, grated or thinly sliced

fresh rosemary sprigs, to garnish

1 Heat 1½ tablespoons oil in a frying pan, add the onions, garlic and pepper and sauté for about 10 minutes, or until softened. Remove the pan from the heat and set aside.

2 Preheat the oven to 200°C/400°F/gas mark 6. Place the maize (corn) meal, potato flour, soya flour, baking powder and salt in a bowl and stir to mix. Lightly rub in the butter until the mixture resembles breadcrumbs, then add enough milk, mixing to make a soft dough.

3 Place the dough on a sheet of non-stick baking paper, then roll or press out to form a 25cm (10in) round, making the edges slightly thicker than the centre. Brush the pizza dough with the remaining oil.

4 Combine the chopped tomatoes, chopped rosemary and seasoning and spread this mixture over the dough. Spoon the onion mixture over the tomatoes and top with the cheese.

5 Bake for 25–30 minutes, or until the pizza base is crisp and golden brown. Garnish with rosemary sprigs and serve immediately, cut into slices, with a mixed green salad.

Banana bread

PREPARATION TIME *20 minutes* COOKING TIME *1–1¼ hours*
MAKES *1 loaf (serves 10)*

115g (4oz) butter, softened

115g (4oz) light soft
brown sugar

115g (4oz) thick-set honey

2 eggs, beaten

225g (8oz) gluten-free plain
white flour

1½ teaspoons gluten-free
baking powder

1 teaspoon ground cinnamon

2 large bananas (total weight
of bananas with skin = about
450g/1lb)

a squeeze of lemon juice

55g (2oz) walnuts, chopped

1 Preheat the oven to 180°C/350°F/gas mark 4. Grease and
line a 900g (2lb) loaf tin and set aside. Place the butter, sugar
and honey in a bowl and beat together until light and fluffy.
Gradually beat in the eggs, then fold in the flour, baking powder
and cinnamon.

2 Peel the bananas and mash the flesh with a little lemon juice.
Fold the mashed bananas and walnuts into the bread mixture
until well mixed, then spoon the mixture into the loaf tin and
level the surface.

3 Bake for 1–1¼ hours, or until risen, golden brown and firm to
touch. Cover loosely with foil towards the end of the cooking
time if the top is browning too quickly.

4 Remove the bread from the oven and allow to cool in the tin
for a few minutes, then turn out onto a wire rack. Serve warm or
cold in slices.

Variation Use pecans, raisins or chopped pitted dried dates in place
of walnuts.

Apple ginger muffins

PREPARATION TIME *20 minutes* **COOKING TIME** *15–20 minutes*
MAKES *8 large or 12 medium-sized muffins*

115g (4oz) gluten-free maize (corn) meal

85g (3oz) rice flour

1 tablespoon gluten-free baking powder

a pinch of salt

1½ teaspoons ground ginger

55g (2oz) butter, melted

55g (2oz) light soft brown sugar

1 egg, beaten

200ml (7fl oz) milk

115g (4oz) cooking apple (peeled & cored weight), chopped

1 Preheat the oven to 200°C/400°F/gas mark 6. Grease 8 or 12 cups of a 12-cup muffin tin or line each cup with a paper muffin case and set aside. Place the maize (corn) meal, rice flour, baking powder, salt and ginger in a bowl and stir to mix.

2 Mix together the melted butter, sugar, egg and milk and pour over the dry ingredients. Fold the ingredients together gently – just enough to combine them. The mixture will look quite lumpy, which is correct as over-mixing will result in heavy muffins.

3 Fold in the chopped apple, then spoon the mixture into the prepared muffin cups, dividing it evenly between each one.

4 Bake the muffins for 15–20 minutes, or until risen and golden brown. Transfer to a wire rack to cool. Serve warm or cold.

Variations Use fresh raspberries or blackberries in place of chopped apple. Use ground cinnamon or mixed spice in place of ginger.

Ginger teabread

PREPARATION TIME *20 minutes, plus cooling* **COOKING TIME** *1–1¼ hours*
MAKES *1 loaf (serves 8–10)*

115g (4oz) light soft brown sugar

85g (3oz) butter

85g (3oz) golden syrup

85g (3oz) black treacle

7 tablespoons milk

1 egg, beaten

175g (6oz) gluten-free plain white flour

55g (2oz) gram (chickpea) flour

1½ teaspoons gluten-free baking powder

a pinch of salt

2 teaspoons ground ginger

1 teaspoon ground cinnamon or mixed spice

1 Preheat the oven to 170°C/325°F/gas mark 3. Grease and line a 900g (2lb) loaf tin and set aside. Place the sugar, butter, syrup and treacle in a saucepan and heat gently until melted and blended, stirring occasionally. Remove the pan from the heat and cool slightly, then stir in the milk and egg.

2 Place the flours, baking powder, salt and ground spices in a bowl and stir to mix. Make a well in the centre, pour in the syrup mixture and beat together until thoroughly mixed. Pour the mixture into the loaf tin.

3 Bake the loaf for 1–1¼ hours, or until firm to the touch – a fine skewer inserted in the centre should come out clean. Remove the teabread from the oven and allow to cool in the tin for a few minutes, then turn out onto a wire rack. Store in an airtight container or wrapped in foil. Serve warm or cold in slices.

Variations Fold 55g (2oz) finely chopped, preserved stem ginger into the raw teabread mixture, if desired. Add 1–2 extra teaspoons of ground ginger for a more pronounced gingery flavour.

Apricot and cranberry teabread

PREPARATION TIME *20 minutes* **COOKING TIME** *1–1¼ hours*
MAKES *1 loaf (serves 10)*

225g (8oz) gluten-free plain white flour

2 teaspoons gluten-free baking powder

115g (4oz) butter, diced

115g (4oz) light soft brown sugar

finely grated zest of 1 small orange

175g (6oz) ready-to-eat dried apricots, chopped

175g (6oz) dried cranberries

2 eggs, beaten

150ml (¼ pint) milk

1 Remove the kneading blade from the bread pan and grease and line the base and sides of the pan. Sift the flour and baking powder into a bowl, then lightly rub in the butter. Stir in the sugar, orange zest and dried fruit. Add the eggs and milk and mix together until thoroughly combined. Spoon the mixture into the pan and level the surface.

2 Place the bread pan in position in the machine and close the lid. Select the Bake Only setting and enter 60 minutes on the timer. Press Start. After baking, a fine skewer inserted in the centre of the teabread should come out clean. If the teabread requires further baking, select the same programme as before and enter a further 10–15 minutes on the timer, or until the teabread is cooked.

3 Remove the bread pan from the machine using oven gloves, then leave to stand for 5 minutes, before turning the teabread out of the pan onto a wire rack to cool. Serve warm or cold in slices.

Variations Use sultanas or dried cherries in place of cranberries. Use the finely grated zest of 1 lemon in place of orange zest.

Speciality & festive breads

Speciality breads are made from
yeasted doughs enriched with a combination of
other ingredients such as eggs, sugar, butter, dried
fruit or chocolate. Enriched breads, both sweet and
savoury, vary in texture from soft and airy loaves with
a rich and buttery flavour, to wonderfully light and
flaky melt-in-the-mouth yeasted pastries. Here
we include a delicious selection of enriched
speciality and celebration breads
from all over the world.

Orange and cinnamon brioche

PREPARATION TIME *30 minutes, plus rising* **COOKING TIME** *40 minutes*
SERVES *12–14*

450g (1lb) strong plain white flour

½ teaspoon salt

1 sachet (7g/¼oz) easy-blend dried yeast

55g (2oz) caster sugar

1 tablespoon finely grated orange zest

1 teaspoon ground cinnamon

150g (5½oz) butter

3 large eggs, lightly beaten

about 3 tablespoons warm milk

beaten egg yolk, to glaze

1 Grease a 1.7 litre (3 pint) brioche tin and set aside. Sift the flour and salt into a bowl, then stir in the yeast, sugar, orange zest and cinnamon. Rub half the butter into the flour mixture, then make a well in the centre. Melt the remaining butter, cool slightly, then add to the flour mixture together with the eggs and enough milk, mixing to form a soft dough.

2 Turn the dough onto a lightly floured surface and knead until smooth and elastic. Shape the dough into a round, then place it in a lightly oiled bowl, cover and leave to rise in a warm place until doubled in size.

3 Knock back the dough on a lightly floured surface, then cut a quarter from the dough and set aside. Knead the remaining large piece of dough, shape it into a large round ball and place it in the brioche tin. Shape the reserved piece of dough into a pear shape.

4 Make a hollow in the centre of the large round of dough and place the thinner end of the pear-shaped piece of dough into the hollow. Cover and leave to rise again for about 30 minutes, or until the dough nearly reaches the top of the tin.

5 Meanwhile, preheat the oven to 200°C/400°F/gas mark 6. Brush the brioche with beaten egg yolk, then bake for about 40 minutes, or until risen and golden. Turn out and cool on a wire rack. Serve warm or cold in slices or wedges.

Rum babas

PREPARATION TIME *40 minutes, plus rising*   COOKING TIME *15–20 minutes*
MAKES *12 babas*

85g (3oz) currants

8 tablespoons dark rum

2 tablespoons boiling water

225g (8oz) strong plain
white flour

½ teaspoon salt

1 sachet (7g/¼oz) easy-blend
dried yeast

15g (½oz) caster sugar

3 tablespoons warm milk

3 large eggs, lightly beaten

115g (4oz) butter, softened

250g (9oz) granulated sugar

1 Grease 12 small baba or dariole moulds (each about 125ml/4fl oz capacity) and set aside. Mix the currants, 4 tablespoons rum and the boiling water together in a small bowl and leave to soak. Sift the flour and salt into a large bowl, then stir in the yeast and caster sugar. Make a well in the centre, then add the milk and eggs and mix to form a smooth, very thick, batter-like dough.

2 Knead the dough in the bowl, beating it with your hand for 4–5 minutes, or until smooth, elastic and slightly stiffer. Cover and leave to rise in a warm place until doubled in size.

3 Knock back the dough in the bowl, then gradually work in the butter and soaked currants (without any remaining soaking liquid, which can be sprinkled over the babas just before serving), until a smooth, even, thick batter is formed. Spoon the mixture into the moulds, filling each one about one-third full. Place on a baking sheet, then cover and leave to rise again for about 30 minutes, or until the mixture almost reaches the top of the moulds.

4 Meanwhile, preheat the oven to 200°C/400°F/gas mark 6. Bake the babas for 15–20 minutes, or until golden. Turn out and cool on a wire rack.

5 Place the granulated sugar and 600ml (1 pint) water in a pan and heat gently until the sugar has dissolved, then bring to the boil and boil rapidly for 5 minutes. Remove the pan from the heat, then add the babas to the hot syrup, one or two at a time, turning them over several times to ensure they absorb the syrup – the babas will swell and look shiny.

6 Lift the babas out of the syrup and place on a plate. Sprinkle the babas with the remaining rum just before serving. Combine any remaining syrup and soaking liquid and spoon over the babas to serve.

Stollen

PREPARATION TIME *30 minutes, plus rising* **COOKING TIME** *40 minutes*
MAKES *1 loaf (serves 10–12)*

350g (12oz) strong plain white flour

½ teaspoon salt

1 teaspoon ground mixed spice

40g (1½oz) butter, diced

25g (1oz) caster sugar

2 teaspoons easy-blend dried yeast

finely grated zest of 1 lemon

175g (6oz) luxury mixed dried fruit

55g (2oz) blanched almonds, finely chopped

1 large egg, lightly beaten

about 125ml (4fl oz) warm milk

175g (6oz) ready-made marzipan or almond paste

icing sugar & ground cinnamon, for dusting

1 Grease a baking sheet and set aside. Sift the flour, salt and mixed spice into a large bowl, then rub in the butter. Stir in the caster sugar, yeast, lemon zest, dried fruit and almonds. Make a well in the centre, then add the egg and enough milk, mixing to form a soft dough.

2 Turn the dough onto a lightly floured surface and knead until smooth and elastic. Shape the dough into a round, place it in a lightly oiled bowl, cover and leave to rise in a warm place until doubled in size.

3 Knock back the dough on a lightly floured surface, then shape into a rectangle about 20 x 10cm (8 x 4in) in size and 2.5cm (1in) thick. Roll the marzipan into a long sausage, just a little shorter than the length of the rectangle.

4 Place the marzipan log along the centre of the dough, fold the dough over almost in half to enclose it, and press the edges together to seal. Transfer to the baking sheet, cover and leave to rise again for 45–60 minutes.

5 Meanwhile, preheat the oven to 180°C/350°F/gas mark 4. Bake the stollen for about 40 minutes, or until it sounds hollow when tapped underneath. Transfer to a wire rack to cool. Dust with a mixture of sifted icing sugar and ground cinnamon. Serve in slices.

Variation Drizzle the baked stollen with a thin glacé icing in place of the dusting of icing sugar and ground cinnamon.

158

Panettone

PREPARATION TIME *25 minutes, plus rising* COOKING TIME *45–50 minutes*
MAKES *1 loaf (serves 8–10)*

350g (12oz) strong plain white flour

¼ teaspoon salt

1 sachet (7g/¼oz) easy-blend dried yeast

55g (2oz) caster sugar

115g (4oz) sultanas

55g (2oz) chopped mixed peel

finely grated zest of 1 small lemon

3 large eggs, lightly beaten

4 tablespoons warm milk

115g (4oz) butter, softened

15g (½oz) butter, melted

1 Grease and line a deep 18cm (7in) round cake tin. Using string, tie a collar of a double layer of greaseproof paper around the outside of the tin, bringing the collar about 7.5cm (3in) above the rim. Set aside.

2 Sift the flour and salt into a bowl, then stir in the yeast, sugar, sultanas, mixed peel and lemon zest. Make a well in the centre, then add the eggs, milk and softened butter and beat the dough for 5 minutes or until it becomes elastic and leaves the sides of the bowl.

3 Turn the dough onto a floured surface and knead until smooth, then shape into a round, place in a lightly oiled bowl, cover and leave to rise in a warm place until doubled in size.

4 Knock back the dough on a lightly floured surface, then shape it into a ball. Place in the prepared tin and cut a cross in the top. Cover and leave to rise again for about 30 minutes, or until doubled in size.

5 Meanwhile, preheat the oven to 200°C/400°F/gas mark 6. Brush the top of the panettone liberally with melted butter. Bake for 15 minutes, then reduce the oven temperature to 180°C/350°F/gas mark 4 and bake for a further 30–35 minutes, or until the top is golden and crisp. Turn out and cool on a wire rack. Cut into wedges to serve.

Easter bread ring

PREPARATION TIME *30 minutes, plus rising* **COOKING TIME** *25 minutes*
MAKES *1 loaf (serves 10–12)*

225g (8oz) strong plain white flour

½ teaspoon salt

55g (2oz) butter, diced

1½ teaspoons easy-blend dried yeast

25g (1oz) caster sugar

1 large egg, lightly beaten

about 100ml (3½fl oz) warm milk, plus extra for glazing

55g (2oz) sultanas

55g (2oz) ready-to-eat dried apricots, chopped

55g (2oz) light soft brown sugar

1½ teaspoons ground mixed spice

115g (4oz) icing sugar, sifted

25g (1oz) toasted flaked almonds

1 Grease a baking sheet and set aside. Sift the flour and salt into a large bowl, then lightly rub in 25g (1oz) of the butter. Stir in the yeast and caster sugar. Make a well in the centre, then add the egg and enough milk, mixing to form a soft dough.

2 Turn the dough onto a lightly floured surface and knead until smooth and elastic. Shape the dough into a round, then place it in a lightly oiled bowl and leave to rise in a warm place until doubled in size.

3 Knock back the dough on a lightly floured surface, then roll it out to form a 46 x 30cm (18 x 12in) rectangle. Melt the remaining butter and brush it over the dough.

4 Combine the sultanas, apricots, soft brown sugar and mixed spice and sprinkle evenly over the dough. Starting from a long side, roll up the dough fairly tightly like a Swiss roll. Make sure the seam is underneath, then shape the dough into a circle. Brush the ends with a little milk and press them together to seal. Place on the baking sheet.

5 Using a sharp knife, cut two-thirds of the way through the dough at 4cm (1½in) intervals. Twist the slices outwards at an angle so they overlap slightly. Cover and leave to rise again for about 1 hour or until doubled in size.

6 Meanwhile, preheat the oven to 200°C/400°F/gas mark 6. Bake the bread ring for about 25 minutes, or until it is risen and golden brown. Transfer to a wire rack to cool.

7 Mix the icing sugar with about 4 teaspoons water to make a thin glacé icing. Drizzle over the warm baked ring and sprinkle with flaked almonds. Serve warm or cold in slices.

Drizzled Danish apple plait

PREPARATION TIME *35 minutes, plus rising* COOKING TIME *25–30 minutes*
SERVES *8*

225g (8oz) strong plain white flour

½ teaspoon salt

25g (1oz) butter, diced

1½ teaspoons easy-blend dried yeast

55g (2oz) caster sugar

1 large egg, lightly beaten

about 100ml (3½fl oz) warm milk

140g (5oz) ready-made marzipan or almond paste, coarsely grated

1 large or 2 small cooking apples, peeled, cored & thinly sliced

1 teaspoon ground cinnamon

beaten egg, to glaze

85g (3oz) icing sugar, sifted

15g (½oz) toasted flaked almonds or chopped pistachio nuts, to decorate

1 Grease a baking sheet and set aside. Sift the flour and salt into a large bowl, then lightly rub in the butter. Stir in the yeast and 25g (1oz) caster sugar. Make a well in the centre, then add the egg and enough milk, mixing to form a soft dough.

2 Turn the dough onto a lightly floured surface and knead until smooth and elastic. Shape into a round, then place in a lightly oiled bowl and leave to rise in a warm place until doubled in size.

3 Knock back the dough on a lightly floured surface, then roll it out to form a 30 x 20cm (12 x 8in) rectangle. Place the marzipan evenly down the centre third (lengthways) of the dough (about 6cm/2½in wide). Toss the apple slices with the remaining caster sugar and cinnamon, then spoon this mixture over the marzipan.

4 On the longest sides of the dough, make diagonal cuts up to the filling at 2.5cm (1in) intervals. Plait the strips of dough over the filling, pressing lightly to seal. Tuck the ends under to seal at the top and bottom of the plait. Place the plait on the baking sheet, then cover and leave to rise again until doubled in size.

5 Preheat the oven to 200°C/400°F/gas mark 6. Lightly brush the plait with beaten egg, then bake for 25–30 minutes, or until risen and golden. Transfer to a wire rack to cool.

6 Blend the icing sugar with a little water to make a thin glacé icing. Drizzle the icing over the warm plait; sprinkle with almonds or pistachio nuts. Serve warm or cold in slices.

Croissants

PREPARATION TIME *45 minutes, plus rising* COOKING TIME *15–20 minutes* MAKES *12 croissants*

500g (1lb 2oz) strong plain white flour

½ teaspoon salt

280g (10oz) butter, at room temperature

1 sachet (7g/¼oz) easy-blend dried yeast

25g (1oz) caster sugar

about 300ml (½ pint) warm milk

beaten egg, to glaze

To make in a breadmachine: use quantities as listed in main recipe but amend following ingredients and use 300ml (½ pint) milk, 1 teaspoon salt and use fast-action dried yeast. Use 55g (2oz) butter in dough; use remaining butter as instructed in Step 3 of main recipe. Add ingredients to breadmachine in order specified in your instruction book. Use Dough setting for this recipe, then continue as above from Step 3 of main recipe.

1 Grease 2 baking sheets and set aside. Sift the flour and salt into a large bowl, then lightly rub in 55g (2oz) butter. Stir in the yeast and sugar. Make a well in the centre, then add enough milk, mixing to form a soft dough.

2 Turn the dough onto a floured surface and knead for 3–4 minutes. Shape into a round, then place in an oiled bowl, cover and leave to rise in a warm place until doubled in size.

3 Knock back the dough on a lightly floured surface, then roll out to form a rectangle about 35 x 18cm (14 x 7in). Flatten the remaining butter into a block about 2cm (¾in) thick. With a short side of the dough rectangle nearest to you, place the butter on top of the dough so that it covers the top two-thirds of the rectangle. Fold the bottom third of the dough over the middle third, then fold the top buttered third down over the top of the middle third to form a parcel. Seal the edges with a rolling pin.

4 Give the dough a quarter turn so the folded side is to the left. Roll into a rectangle as before, then fold the bottom third up and the top third down and seal the edges, as before. Wrap in greaseproof paper and chill in the refrigerator for 20 minutes. Repeat the rolling, folding and chilling twice more, turning the dough 90 degrees each time.

5 Roll out the dough on a lightly floured surface to form a 53 x 35cm (21 x 14in) rectangle and cut into 12 equal triangles. Roll each triangle into a sausage shape, starting from the long side and ending with the point of the triangle. Bend the ends of each croissant round to give a crescent or half-moon shape. Place on the baking sheets. Cover and leave to rise again for about 30 minutes, or until almost doubled in size.

6 Preheat the oven to 220°C/425°F/gas mark 7. Lightly brush the croissants with beaten egg and bake for 20 minutes. Serve warm.

Doughnuts

PREPARATION TIME *35 minutes, plus rising* **COOKING TIME** *25 minutes* **MAKES** *16 doughnuts*

500g (1lb 2oz) strong plain white flour

½ teaspoon salt

25g (1oz) butter, diced

2 teaspoons easy-blend dried yeast

175g (6oz) caster sugar

2 large eggs, lightly beaten

about 175ml (6fl oz) warm milk

115g (4oz) strawberry or raspberry jam

sunflower oil, for deep-frying

1½ teaspoons ground cinnamon

To make in a breadmachine: use quantities as listed in main recipe but amend following ingredients and use 175ml (6fl oz) milk, 1 teaspoon salt and 1½ teaspoons fast-action dried yeast. Use 85g (3oz) caster sugar in dough; use remaining sugar as instructed in Step 7 of main recipe. Add ingredients to breadmachine in order specified in your instruction book. Use Dough setting for this recipe, then continue as above from Step 3 of main recipe.

1 Oil 2 baking sheets and set aside. Sift the flour and salt into a large bowl, then lightly rub in the butter. Stir in the yeast and 85g (3oz) sugar. Make a well in the centre, then stir in the eggs and enough milk, mixing to form a soft dough.

2 Turn the dough onto a floured surface and knead until smooth. Shape into a round, then place in a lightly oiled bowl, cover and leave to rise in a warm place until doubled in size.

3 Knock back the dough on a lightly floured surface, then divide into 16 equal pieces. Shape each piece of dough into a ball, then flatten each one into a disc about 1cm (½in) thick.

4 Place 1 heaped teaspoon of jam into the middle of each piece of dough, gather the edges of the dough up and over the jam, enclosing it completely, then pinch the edges firmly together to seal, and roll into a ball. Place the doughnuts on the baking sheets, cover and leave to rise again for about 30 minutes, or until almost doubled in size.

5 Heat some oil in a deep-fat fryer to 170°C/325°F and cook the doughnuts in batches in the hot oil for about 6 minutes, or until golden all over, turning once.

6 Remove the doughnuts from the fryer using a slotted spoon and drain on kitchen paper.

7 Combine the remaining sugar and cinnamon in a bowl and toss the doughnuts in the sugar mixture, coating them all over. Serve immediately.

Devonshire splits

PREPARATION TIME *25 minutes, plus rising* **COOKING TIME** *15 minutes*
MAKES *10 Devonshire splits*

350g (12oz) strong plain white flour

½ teaspoon salt

40g (1½oz) butter, diced

1½ teaspoons easy-blend dried yeast

40g (1½oz) caster sugar

about 200ml (7fl oz) warm milk

strawberry or raspberry jam & clotted cream, to serve

sifted icing sugar, for dusting

1 Grease 2 baking sheets and set aside. Sift the flour and salt into a large bowl, then lightly rub in the butter. Stir in the yeast and caster sugar. Make a well in the centre, then add enough milk, mixing to form a soft dough.

2 Turn the dough onto a lightly floured surface and knead until smooth and elastic. Shape the dough into a round, then place it in a lightly oiled bowl, cover and leave to rise in a warm place until doubled in size.

3 Knock back the dough on a lightly floured surface, then divide into 10 equal portions and roll each portion into a ball. Place the dough balls on the baking sheets and flatten them slightly. Cover and leave to rise again until doubled in size.

4 Meanwhile, preheat the oven to 220°C/425°F/gas mark 7. Bake the buns for about 15 minutes, or until they feel soft and sound hollow when tapped underneath. Transfer to a wire rack to cool.

5 Split each bun at an angle and fill with jam and cream. Dust with sifted icing sugar just before serving.

To make in a breadmachine: use quantities as listed in main recipe but amend following ingredients and use 210ml (7½fl oz) milk and use fast-action dried yeast. Add ingredients to breadmachine in order specified in your instruction book. Use Dough setting for this recipe, then continue as above from Step 3 of main recipe.

Chelsea buns

PREPARATION TIME *30 minutes, plus rising* COOKING TIME *30 minutes*
MAKES *12 buns*

225g (8oz) strong plain white flour

½ teaspoon salt

55g (2oz) butter, diced

1½ teaspoons easy-blend dried yeast

25g (1oz) caster sugar

1 large egg, lightly beaten

about 100ml (3½fl oz) warm milk

85g (3oz) mixed raisins & currants

55g (2oz) sultanas

55g (2oz) light soft brown sugar

1½ teaspoons ground cinnamon

2 tablespoons clear honey, to glaze

1 Grease an 18cm (7in) square cake tin and set aside. Sift the flour and salt into a large bowl, then lightly rub in 25g (1oz) butter. Stir in the yeast and caster sugar. Make a well in the centre, then add the egg and enough milk, mixing to form a soft dough.

2 Turn the dough onto a floured surface and knead until smooth. Shape into a round, then place in a lightly oiled bowl, cover and leave to rise in a warm place until doubled in size.

3 Knock back the dough on a lightly floured surface, then roll out to form a 30 x 23cm (12 x 9in) rectangle. Melt the remaining butter and brush it over the dough.

4 Combine the dried fruit, brown sugar and cinnamon and sprinkle over the dough.

5 Starting from a long side, roll up the dough fairly tightly like a Swiss roll. Cut into 12 even slices, then place the rolls, cut-side up, in the tin. Cover and leave to rise in a warm place until doubled in size.

6 Meanwhile, preheat the oven to 190°C/375°F/gas mark 5. Bake the buns for about 20–25 minutes, or until risen and golden brown.

7 Remove from the oven and brush twice with honey while still hot. Cool slightly in the tin, then turn out onto a wire rack. Serve warm or cold.

To make in a breadmachine: use quantities as listed in main recipe but amend following ingredients and use 100ml (3½fl oz) milk and 1 teaspoon fast-action dried yeast. Use 25g (1oz) butter in dough; use remaining butter as instructed in Step 3 of main recipe. Add ingredients to breadmachine in order specified in your instruction book. Use Dough setting; continue from Step 3 of main recipe.

171

Danish pastries

PREPARATION TIME *50 minutes, plus rising* **COOKING TIME** *15–20 minutes* **MAKES** *16 pastries*

500g (1lb 2oz) strong plain white flour

½ teaspoon salt

350g (12oz) butter, at room temperature

2 teaspoons easy-blend dried yeast

55g (2oz) caster sugar

2 large eggs, lightly beaten

about 200ml (7fl oz) warm milk

175g (6oz) ready-made almond paste or marzipan

16 apricot halves (canned or fresh)

beaten egg, to glaze

115g (4oz) icing sugar, sifted

1 Grease 2 baking sheets; set aside. Sift the flour and salt into a bowl; rub in 55g (2oz) butter. Stir in the yeast and caster sugar. Mix in the eggs and enough milk to form a soft dough.

2 Turn the dough onto a floured surface and knead until smooth. Shape into a round, then place in a lightly oiled bowl, cover and leave to rise in a warm place until doubled in size.

3 Knock back the dough, then roll out to a rectangle about 35 x 20cm (14 x 8in) in size. With a short side of the rectangle nearest to you, dot the top two-thirds of the dough with half of the remaining butter. Fold the bottom third of the dough up over the middle third, then fold the top third down over the top of the middle third to form a parcel. Seal the edges.

4 Give the dough a quarter turn so the folded side is to the left. Roll out to a rectangle, as before. Dot with the remaining butter and fold as before, then wrap in greaseproof paper and chill in the refrigerator for 15 minutes. Roll, fold and chill the dough twice more, turning the dough a quarter turn each time.

5 Divide the dough into 4 equal portions, then roll each one out on a floured surface to form a 20cm (8in) square. Cut each square into quarters. Place a round of almond paste in the middle of each square, then fold 2 opposite corners of each square into the middle and press to seal. Top the centre of each with an apricot half, cut-side down. Place on the baking sheets, cover and leave to rise for about 30 minutes, or until almost doubled in size.

6 Preheat the oven to 220°C/425°F/gas mark 7. Lightly brush the pastries with beaten egg, then bake for 15–20 minutes, or until crisp and golden brown. Transfer to a wire rack.

7 Blend the icing sugar with 3–4 teaspoons water to make a thin glacé icing, then drizzle a little icing over each pastry while still warm. Leave to cool and serve warm or cold.

Pecan scroll

PREPARATION TIME *35 minutes, plus rising* **COOKING TIME** *30–40 minutes*
MAKES *1 loaf (serves 10–12)*

450g (1lb) strong plain
white flour

1 teaspoon salt

1 sachet (7g/¼oz) easy-blend
dried yeast

175g (6oz) caster sugar

100g (3½oz) butter, melted

about 175ml (6fl oz)
warm milk

115g (4oz) pecan nuts, ground
or finely chopped

55g (2oz) plain cake crumbs

1 large egg, lightly beaten

½ teaspoon ground cinnamon

85g (3oz) icing sugar

pecan nuts, to decorate

1 Grease a 900g (2lb) loaf tin and set aside. Sift the flour and
salt into a large bowl, then stir in the yeast and 85g (3oz) caster
sugar. Make a well in the centre, then add 85g (3oz) melted
butter and enough milk, mixing to form a soft dough.
2 Turn the dough onto a lightly floured surface and knead until
smooth and elastic. Shape the dough into a round, then place
it in a lightly oiled bowl, cover and leave to rise in a warm place
until doubled in size.
3 Knock back the dough on a lightly floured surface, then roll
it out to form a rectangle about 30 x 20cm (12 x 8in) in size.
Combine the remaining caster sugar, ground or chopped pecan
nuts, cake crumbs and egg in a bowl, then spread this mixture
over the dough.
4 Roll up the dough from each short edge to the centre to make
a scroll shape. Place in the loaf tin, scroll-side (crack-side) up, re-
shaping it slightly to fit in the tin. Cover and leave to rise again
for about 30 minutes, or until it just reaches the top of the tin.
5 Meanwhile, preheat the oven to 200°C/400°F/gas mark 6. Bake
the scroll for 30–40 minutes, or until risen and golden brown.
Turn out, then invert onto a wire rack, so the scroll shape is
uppermost. Brush the remaining melted butter all over the loaf,
then sprinkle with cinnamon. Leave to cool.
6 Blend the icing sugar with 2–3 teaspoons water to make a thin
glacé icing. Drizzle the icing over the scroll, decorate with pecan
nuts and leave to set. Serve in slices.

Irish barm brack

PREPARATION TIME *25 minutes, plus rising* **COOKING TIME** *45 minutes*
MAKES *1 loaf (serves 8–10)*

450g (1lb) strong plain white flour

½ teaspoon salt

2 teaspoons easy-blend dried yeast

55g (2oz) caster sugar

115g (4oz) sultanas

115g (4oz) currants

1½ teaspoons ground cinnamon

55g (2oz) butter, softened

1 egg, lightly beaten

about 175ml (6fl oz) warm milk

1 tablespoon granulated sugar

2 tablespoons boiling water

1 Grease a deep 20cm (8in) round cake tin and set aside. Sift the flour and salt into a large bowl, then stir in the yeast, caster sugar, dried fruit and cinnamon. Make a well in the centre, then add the butter, egg and enough milk, mixing to form a soft dough.

2 Turn the dough onto a lightly floured surface and knead until smooth and elastic. Shape the dough into a round, then place it in a lightly oiled bowl, cover and leave to rise in a warm place until doubled in size.

3 Knock back the dough on a lightly floured surface, then shape into a round and place in the cake tin. Cover and leave to rise again until doubled in size.

4 Meanwhile, preheat the oven to 200°C/400°F/gas mark 6. Bake the loaf for about 45 minutes, or until it is golden brown and sounds hollow when tapped underneath, covering it loosely with foil towards the end of the cooking time if the top is browning too quickly.

5 Meanwhile, dissolve the granulated sugar in the boiling water. When the loaf is baked, brush with the sugar glaze, then return it to the oven for a further 1–2 minutes. Turn out and cool on a wire rack. Serve in slices on its own or buttered.

Variations *Replace 55g (2oz) sultanas with chopped mixed peel, if desired. Use raisins in place of currants.*

Teacake fingers

PREPARATION TIME *25 minutes, plus rising* **COOKING TIME** *20 minutes*
MAKES *12 teacake fingers*

500g (1lb 2oz) packet white bread mix

55g (2oz) butter, diced

25g (1oz) caster sugar

115g (4oz) sultanas

55g (2oz) chopped mixed peel

150ml (¼ pint) warm milk

about 150ml (¼ pint) warm water

beaten egg, to glaze

1 Grease 2 baking sheets and set aside. Place the bread mix in a large bowl, then lightly rub in the butter. Stir in the sugar, sultanas and mixed peel, then add the milk and enough water, mixing to form a soft dough.

2 Turn the dough onto a lightly floured surface and knead until smooth and elastic. Divide the dough into 12 equal pieces. Roll and shape each piece of dough into a long roll or finger shape and place on the baking sheets. Cover and leave to rise in a warm place until doubled in size.

3 Meanwhile, preheat the oven to 190°C/375°F/gas mark 5. Brush the teacakes with beaten egg, then bake them for about 20 minutes, or until risen and golden brown. Transfer to a wire rack to cool. Serve split, lightly toasted and spread with butter.

Variations Add 1–2 teaspoons ground mixed spice to the bread mix, for extra flavour, if desired. Use currants or raisins in place of mixed peel.

Pesto Parmesan pull-apart

PREPARATION TIME *30 minutes, plus rising* **COOKING TIME** *30–35 minutes*
SERVES *16*

450g (1lb) strong plain white flour

1 teaspoon salt

1½ teaspoons easy-blend dried yeast

1 teaspoon caster sugar

about 300ml (½ pint) warm water

3 tablespoons green pesto sauce

40g (1½oz) fresh Parmesan cheese, grated

beaten egg, to glaze

1 Grease a deep 23cm (9in) round cake tin and set aside. Sift the flour and salt into a bowl, then stir in the yeast and sugar. Mix in enough water to form a soft dough.

2 Turn the dough onto a floured surface and knead until smooth. Shape into a round, then place in an oiled bowl, cover and leave to rise in a warm place until doubled in size.

3 Knock back the dough on a floured surface, then roll out to form a 40 x 28cm (16 x 11in) rectangle. Spread the pesto sauce over the dough, then sprinkle with Parmesan cheese.

4 Starting from a long side, roll up the dough fairly tightly like a Swiss roll. Cut into 16 even slices, then place the rolls, cut-side up, in a circular pattern in the cake tin. Cover and leave to rise again for about 30 minutes, or until doubled in size.

5 Preheat the oven to 200°C/400°F/gas mark 6. Brush the spirals with beaten egg, then bake for 30–35 minutes, or until deep golden brown. Cool slightly in the tin, then turn out onto a wire rack to cool completely. Pull the rolls apart to serve. Serve warm or cold.

To make in a breadmachine: use quantities as listed in main recipe but amend following ingredients and use 315ml (10½fl oz) water, 1¼ teaspoons salt, 1½ teaspoons caster sugar and use fast-action dried yeast. Add ingredients to breadmachine in order specified in your instruction book. Use Dough setting for this recipe, then continue as above from Step 3 of main recipe.

Bread dishes

As well as being delicious
in its own right, bread can also be used as
a versatile ingredient in many sweet and savoury
dishes. Some of the classic, everyday recipes in this
chapter will be familiar to you, whereas other more
creative recipes may be less so. From classic French
Toast and Welsh Rarebit to Summer Pudding and
Treacle Lattice Tart, we include a tempting
selection of tasty recipes, all of which
use bread as an ingredient.

Grilled vegetable bruschetta

PREPARATION TIME *15 minutes* **COOKING TIME** *15 minutes*
SERVES *4 (makes 8 bruschetta)*

1 red or yellow pepper, seeded
& sliced into strips

1 courgette, halved & thinly
sliced lengthways

1 red onion, thinly sliced

2 large plum or vine tomatoes,
thickly sliced

1 tablespoon olive oil, plus
extra for drizzling

2 teaspoons (gluten-free)
wholegrain mustard

sea salt & freshly ground black
pepper, to taste

1 ciabatta loaf, cut into 8 equal
portions (or 8 slices from a
large French baguette or
white flute) or 8 slices of
gluten-free bread

1 clove garlic, halved

shredded fresh basil leaves,
to garnish

1 Preheat the grill to high and line the grill rack with foil. Place
the pepper, courgette, onion and tomatoes in a large bowl.
Whisk together the oil, mustard and seasoning, then drizzle this
mixture over the vegetables and toss gently to mix.
2 Spread the vegetables in a single layer on the grill rack. Grill
for 4–5 minutes on each side, or until lightly browned. Set aside
and keep warm. (If your grill pan is not big enough to grill all
the vegetables at one time, do this stage in 2 batches and keep
the first batch of grilled vegetables warm while grilling the
second batch.)
3 Toast the bread slices on both sides under the grill and, while
still hot, rub the garlic halves over one side of each piece of
toast. Divide the grilled vegetables between the toast slices,
piling them onto the garlicky sides.
4 Drizzle a little olive oil over each slice of bruschetta, garnish
with shredded basil and serve immediately with a mixed
leaf salad.

French onion soup

PREPARATION TIME *20 minutes* **COOKING TIME** *1 hour 5 minutes*
SERVES *6*

85g (3oz) butter

900g (2lb) onions, thinly sliced

1 tablespoon caster sugar

25g (1oz) plain white flour

200ml (7fl oz) dry white wine

1.4 litres (2½ pints) vegetable
or beef stock

sea salt & freshly ground black
pepper

6 slices of bread from a French
baguette

55g (2oz) Gruyère cheese,
grated

1 Melt the butter in a large saucepan. Add the onions and sauté
for about 5 minutes, or until softened. Sprinkle over the sugar
and continue cooking over a low heat, stirring occasionally,
for about 25 minutes, or until the onions are soft, golden
and caramelised.

2 Sprinkle the flour over the onions and cook for 1 minute,
stirring continuously. Stir in the wine and let it bubble until
reduced by half, then stir in the stock and seasoning. Bring to
the boil, stirring, then reduce the heat, cover and simmer for
about 35 minutes, stirring occasionally.

3 Meanwhile, make the Gruyère cheese croûtes. Preheat the grill
to high. Toast the baguette slices on one side, turn them over
and sprinkle the Gruyère cheese evenly on top of each slice. Cook
under the grill until the cheese has melted and is gently bubbling.

4 Ladle the soup into warmed bowls and float a gruyère croûte
on top of each portion of soup. Serve immediately.

*Variation If desired, once the soup is cooked, cool slightly, then purée
about one third of the soup in a blender until smooth. Return the puréed
soup to the soup in the pan and re-heat gently before serving. Alternatively,
purée all the cooked soup and re-heat before serving.*

Melba toast

PREPARATION TIME *10 minutes* **COOKING TIME** *10 minutes*
SERVES *4–6*

**4 thick slices of white or
wholemeal bread**

1 Preheat the grill to high. Toast the bread slices on both sides.
Quickly cut off and discard the crusts using a serrated knife, then
slide the knife between the toasted edges and split each slice
horizontally in half.
2 Cut each piece of bread into 4 triangles, then place them
under the grill again, untoasted-side uppermost, and grill until
golden and crispy and the edges begin to curl.
3 Serve immediately or allow to cool, then store in an airtight
container until ready to use. Warm through in the oven
before serving.

Variation *Sprinkle the cut sides of toast with a little finely grated fresh
Parmesan cheese, before toasting again, if desired.*

French toast

PREPARATION TIME *10 minutes* **COOKING TIME** *10–15 minutes*
SERVES *2–4*

4 slices of white standard or gluten-free bread

2 eggs

150ml (¼ pint) milk

a good pinch of freshly grated nutmeg or ground cinnamon

55g (2oz) butter

1–2 tablespoons sunflower oil

caster sugar, for sprinkling

1 Trim the crusts from the bread slices and discard. Cut each slice of bread into 4 even fingers. Beat the eggs, milk and nutmeg or cinnamon together in a bowl. Dip the bread fingers into this mixture, coating them all over.

2 Melt half the butter with 1 tablespoon oil in a large, heavy-based frying pan. When the butter is foaming, add half the bread fingers and fry until golden brown, turning once.

3 Remove the bread fingers from the pan, drain on kitchen paper and keep hot. Add the remaining butter to the pan with more oil, if needed. Add the remaining bread fingers and fry as before, then drain.

4 Serve the French toast hot, sprinkled with a little caster sugar.

Croque monsieur

PREPARATION TIME *10 minutes* **COOKING TIME** *4–6 minutes*
SERVES *4*

about 55g (2oz) butter,
softened, for spreading

8 thin slices of white standard
or gluten-free bread

4 slices of lean smoked
cooked ham

4 slices of Gruyère or Edam
cheese

freshly ground black pepper,
to taste

fresh flat-leaf parsley sprigs,
to garnish

1 Preheat the grill to high. Butter one side of each bread
slice. Use the bread slices to make 4 sandwiches, making each
sandwich with a slice of ham and a slice of cheese inside,
seasoned with black pepper. Press well together.
2 Toast the sandwiches under the grill until golden-brown on
both sides, turning once.
3 Cut the sandwiches in half diagonally, garnish with parsley
sprigs and serve immediately.

Welsh rarebit

PREPARATION TIME *15 minutes* **COOKING TIME** *10 minutes*
SERVES *4*

115g (4oz) Cheddar cheese, grated

115g (4oz) Gruyère cheese, grated

2–3 teaspoons French or Dijon mustard

1 egg, beaten

2 tablespoons beer

a good pinch of cayenne pepper

sea salt & freshly ground black pepper

4 thick slices of white or brown bread

softened butter, for spreading

chopped fresh parsley, to garnish

1 Preheat the grill to high. Combine the two cheeses in a bowl, then reserve 3–4 tablespoons and set this aside. Add the mustard, egg, beer, cayenne pepper and salt and black pepper to the cheese in the bowl and mix well.

2 Toast the bread on both sides under the grill, then spread the toast with a little butter. Spoon the cheese mixture on to the buttered sides of the toast, dividing it between each one and spreading it evenly, making sure all the edges are covered. Sprinkle over the reserved cheese and grill until lightly browned and bubbling.

3 Sprinkle the rarebits with chopped parsley and serve immediately on their own or with a mixed dark leaf salad.

Garden vegetable pasta bake

PREPARATION TIME *25 minutes* **COOKING TIME** *20 minutes*
SERVES *4*

225g (8oz) dried short-cut macaroni

sea salt & freshly ground black pepper

225g (8oz) small broccoli florets

225g (8oz) courgettes, sliced

55g (2oz) butter

55g (2oz) plain white flour

850ml (1½ pints) milk

175g (6oz) mature Cheddar cheese, grated

1 teaspoon Dijon mustard

2 tablespoons chopped fresh parsley

3 tablespoons fresh white or wholemeal breadcrumbs

fresh parsley sprigs, to garnish

1 Preheat the oven to 200ºC/400ºF/gas mark 6. Grease an ovenproof dish and set aside. Cook the macaroni in a saucepan of lightly salted, boiling water for about 10 minutes, or until just tender. Drain thoroughly, keep warm and set aside.

2 Meanwhile, cook the broccoli and courgettes in a saucepan of boiling water for 3–4 minutes, or until just tender. Drain well and keep warm.

3 Place the butter, flour and milk in a saucepan and heat gently, whisking continuously, until the sauce comes to the boil and thickens. Simmer gently for 2–3 minutes, stirring.

4 Remove the pan from the heat and stir in 140g (5oz) cheese, the mustard, chopped parsley and seasoning. Add the macaroni and vegetables and stir gently to mix. Transfer to the ovenproof dish.

5 Mix the remaining cheese and breadcrumbs together and sprinkle over the macaroni.

6 Bake for about 20 minutes, or until golden brown and bubbling. Garnish with parsley sprigs and serve with fresh crusty bread and a mixed garden salad.

Variations Use sliced mushrooms in place of the courgettes. Use Red Leicester or Gruyère cheese in place of Cheddar.

Apricot bread and butter pudding

PREPARATION TIME *15 minutes, plus 30 minutes standing* **COOKING TIME** *45 minutes*
SERVES *4–6*

6 medium slices of white or wholemeal bread

55g (2oz) butter, softened

115g (4oz) ready-to-eat dried apricots, finely chopped

40g (1½oz) light soft brown sugar

1½ teaspoons ground mixed spice

2 eggs

600ml (1 pint) milk

1 Lightly grease an ovenproof dish and set aside. Spread one side of each bread slice with butter, then cut each slice into 4 triangles. Arrange half of the bread triangles in the base of the ovenproof dish, buttered-side up. Sprinkle the apricots over the top.

2 Mix together the sugar and mixed spice and sprinkle half of this over the apricots. Arrange the remaining bread triangles over the top, buttered-side up, then sprinkle with the remaining sugar and spice mixture.

3 Beat together the eggs and milk and pour evenly over the bread. Set aside for 30 minutes to allow the bread to absorb some of the liquid.

4 Meanwhile, preheat the oven to 180°C/350°F/gas mark 4. Bake the bread pudding for about 45 minutes, or until lightly set and golden brown. Serve warm or cold on its own or with custard, cream or ice cream.

Variations Use sultanas or raisins in place of dried apricots. Use ground cinnamon in place of mixed spice.

Yummy chocolate bread pudding

PREPARATION TIME *25 minutes, plus 30 minutes standing* **COOKING TIME** *45 minutes*
SERVES *4–6*

115g (4oz) plain chocolate, broken into squares

85g (3oz) butter, softened

6 medium slices of white bread

115g (4oz) raisins

600ml (1 pint) milk

2 tablespoons cocoa powder, sifted

25g (1oz) caster sugar

3 eggs

grated plain chocolate, to serve (optional)

Variations Use sliced brioche or fruit bread in place of white bread. Use sultanas, dried cherries or chopped ready-to-eat dried apricots in place of raisins.

1 Grease a 1.5 litre (2¾ pint) ovenproof dish and set aside. Place the squares of chocolate and 25g (1oz) butter in a small heatproof bowl. Place the bowl over a saucepan of simmering water and leave until the mixture is melted and combined, stirring once or twice. Remove from the heat.

2 Thickly spread one side of each slice of bread with the remaining butter. Spread the melted chocolate mixture on top. Cut the bread into small triangles or squares. Place one third of the bread triangles, chocolate-side up, in the ovenproof dish.

3 Sprinkle with half the raisins. Top with another third of the bread triangles, then sprinkle with the remaining raisins. Top with the remaining bread triangles, chocolate-side up.

4 Pour 150ml (¼ pint) milk into a saucepan and heat gently until almost boiling. Remove the pan from the heat, then whisk the cocoa powder and sugar into the hot milk until well mixed. Pour the hot chocolate milk into a jug and whisk in the remaining cold milk.

5 Beat the eggs and chocolate milk together, then strain into the dish over the bread. Leave to stand for 30 minutes, to allow the bread to absorb some of the liquid.

6 Meanwhile, preheat the oven to 180°C/350°F/gas mark 4. Bake the bread pudding for about 45 minutes, or until lightly set. Sprinkle with grated chocolate, if desired, and serve with cream, crème fraîche or Greek-style natural yoghurt.

Traditional Christmas pudding

PREPARATION TIME *30 minutes*   **COOKING TIME** *5–6 hours initial steaming, plus 2–4 hours further steaming*
MAKES *1 pudding (serves 6–8)*

225g (8oz) fresh white breadcrumbs

55g (2oz) plain white flour

225g (8oz) shredded suet

225g (8oz) light soft brown sugar

225g (8oz) sultanas

225g (8oz) currants

55g (2oz) mixed peel

55g (2oz) flaked or chopped almonds

finely grated zest & juice of 1 lemon

1 apple or carrot, peeled (cored) & grated

4 eggs, beaten

3 tablespoons sherry, rum or brandy

1 Grease a 1.4–1.5 litre (2½–2¾ pint) heatproof pudding basin, line the base with non-stick baking paper and set aside. Place the breadcrumbs, flour, suet, sugar, sultanas, currants, mixed peel, almonds, lemon zest and juice and grated apple or carrot in a large bowl and stir until well mixed.

2 Add the eggs to the fruit mixture together with the sherry, rum or brandy and mix thoroughly.

3 Fill the basin with the mixture, pressing down well. Cover the surface of the pudding with a disc of greaseproof paper, then cover the basin with greaseproof paper and foil, pleat them in the centre and secure under the rim with string.

4 Place the basin in the top of a steamer. Steam the pudding over a pan of gently simmering water for 5–6 hours (remember to top up the boiling water periodically so that the pan doesn't boil dry).

5 Remove the steamed pudding from the steamer and set aside to cool completely. Once cold, re-cover the pudding with fresh greaseproof paper and foil and store in a cool, dry, dark place for 6–8 weeks.

6 On Christmas Day, steam the pudding, as before, for 2–4 hours. Turn out the pudding onto a warmed serving plate, cut into wedges and serve with brandy butter or brandy sauce.

Summer pudding

PREPARATION TIME *30 minutes, plus chilling* COOKING TIME *10 minutes*
SERVES *6–8*

500g (1lb 2oz) mixed summer fruits such as blackcurrants, blueberries, loganberries, redcurrants & cherries (pitted)

115g (4oz) caster sugar

280g (10oz) raspberries

2 tablespoons crème de cassis (blackcurrant) or framboise (raspberry) liqueur

8 medium slices of wholemeal or white bread (one day old), crusts removed

fresh redcurrant sprigs & mint leaves, to decorate

1 Place the mixed fruits in a saucepan with the sugar and 5 tablespoons water. Bring gently to the boil, stirring until the sugar has dissolved, then simmer gently for about 5 minutes, or until the juices begin to run and the fruit is just tender. Remove the pan from the heat, stir in the raspberries and liqueur and set aside.

2 Cut a round from one slice of bread to fit the bottom of a 1.2 litre (2 pint) pudding basin and use this to line the bottom of the basin. Cut the remaining bread slices in half, reserve 4 halves for the top and use the rest to line the sides of the basin, making sure the bread fits snugly together, leaving no gaps.

3 Reserve about 125ml (4fl oz) of the fruit juices, then spoon all the fruit and remaining juices into the bread-lined basin. Cover the top of the fruit completely with the reserved bread slices, pressing down lightly and shaping the bread to fit.

4 Cover the pudding with a saucer that is small enough to just fit inside the top of the basin, then set a 450g (1lb) weight (a large can of food is ideal) on top of the saucer. Cool, then chill in the refrigerator for about 8 hours or overnight.

5 Remove the weight and saucer and loosen around the edges of the pudding using a blunt knife. Place a serving plate on top of the basin, hold the two firmly and invert the pudding onto the plate, shaking the basin sharply a couple of times to release the pudding.

6 Spoon a little of the reserved juices over the pudding, concentrating on pale patches, then decorate with redcurrant sprigs and mint leaves. Cut into wedges to serve and spoon any remaining juices over each portion. Serve with whipped cream or crème fraîche.

Treacle lattice tart

PREPARATION TIME *25 minutes* **COOKING TIME** *35 minutes*
SERVES *8*

500g (1lb 2oz) ready-made shortcrust pastry

350g (12oz) golden syrup

25g (1oz) butter

finely grated zest & juice of 1 lemon

200g (7oz) fresh white or brown breadcrumbs

a little milk, for glazing

1 Preheat the oven to 190ºC/375ºF/gas mark 5. Roll out the pastry on a lightly floured surface and use it to line a 25cm (10in) loose-bottomed flan tin. Set aside. Reserve the pastry trimmings.

2 Gently heat the syrup in a saucepan with the butter and lemon zest and juice, until melted and combined, stirring. Remove the pan from the heat, then stir in the breadcrumbs, mixing well. Spoon the breadcrumb mixture into the pastry case and level the surface.

3 Roll out and make strips from the leftover pastry trimmings and place these over the tart in a lattice pattern (twisting them as you go, if desired), brushing the ends with milk so they stick to the pastry case. Brush the pastry lattice with a little milk, if desired.

4 Bake the tart for about 35 minutes, or until the pastry is golden brown and the filling is just set. Cool in the tin for a few minutes, then turn out onto a serving plate. Cut into slices and serve warm or cold with whipped cream, ice cream or custard.

Apple and cinnamon brown betty

PREPARATION TIME *25 minutes* **COOKING TIME** *50 minutes*
SERVES *6*

40g (1½oz) butter

175g (6oz) fresh white or brown standard or gluten-free breadcrumbs

900g (2lb) cooking apples, peeled, cored & thinly sliced

100g (3½oz) caster sugar

1 tablespoon apple juice

2 teaspoons ground cinnamon

1–2 tablespoons demerara sugar

1 Preheat the oven to 200°C/400°F/gas mark 6. Grease a deep 1.7 litre (3 pint) ovenproof soufflé dish (about 18cm/7in in diameter). Melt the butter in a frying pan over a medium heat, add the breadcrumbs and cook for about 5 minutes, or until the crumbs are crisp and golden, stirring. Remove the pan from the heat and set aside.

2 Place the apples in a bowl, add the caster sugar, apple juice and cinnamon. Toss to mix.

3 Spoon one-quarter of the breadcrumb mixture over the base of the ovenproof dish, spreading it evenly. Spoon half of the apple mixture into the dish and cover with another quarter of the breadcrumb mixture.

4 Spoon the remaining apple mixture and any juices over the breadcrumbs, then finally cover with the remaining breadcrumbs. Sprinkle with the demerara sugar.

5 Cover the dish with foil and bake for 20 minutes. Remove the foil and bake for a further 30 minutes, or until the apples are tender and the topping is golden brown. Serve hot on its own or with whipped cream, ice cream or custard.

Variations Use other prepared sliced fresh fruits such as pears or plums in place of apples. Use ground ginger or mixed spice in place of cinnamon.

Brown bread ice cream

PREPARATION TIME *20 minutes, plus freezing* COOKING TIME *10 minutes*
SERVES *4–6*

140g (5oz) fresh wholemeal breadcrumbs

55g (2oz) light soft brown sugar

425ml (¾ pint) ready-made cold custard (standard or low-fat)

150ml (¼ pint) Greek-style natural yoghurt

finely grated zest & juice of 1 lemon

25g (1oz) icing sugar, sifted

thinly pared lemon zest, to decorate

1 Preheat the oven to 200°C/400°F/gas mark 6. Grease a baking sheet. Spread the breadcrumbs over the baking sheet and sprinkle the brown sugar over the top. Bake for about 10 minutes, stirring occasionally, until the sugar caramelises and the breadcrumbs are crisp. Remove from the oven and set aside to cool. Once cool, break up the crumbs roughly with a fork and set aside.

2 Combine the custard, yoghurt, finely grated lemon zest and juice and icing sugar in a bowl, mixing well. Pour the mixture into a chilled, shallow plastic container, spreading it evenly. Cover and freeze for about 1½–2 hours, or until the mixture is mushy in consistency.

3 Turn the mixture into a chilled bowl and beat with a fork or whisk to break down the ice crystals. Fold in the toasted breadcrumbs evenly. Return the mixture to the container and freeze until firm.

4 Transfer the ice cream to the refrigerator for about 30 minutes before serving, to soften slightly. Serve in scoops. Decorate with thinly pared lemon zest and serve with chocolate wafers or scrolls or fresh fruit such as raspberries.

Variations Use double cream, whipped until it forms soft peaks, in place of the Greek-style yoghurt, if desired.

Index

Notes